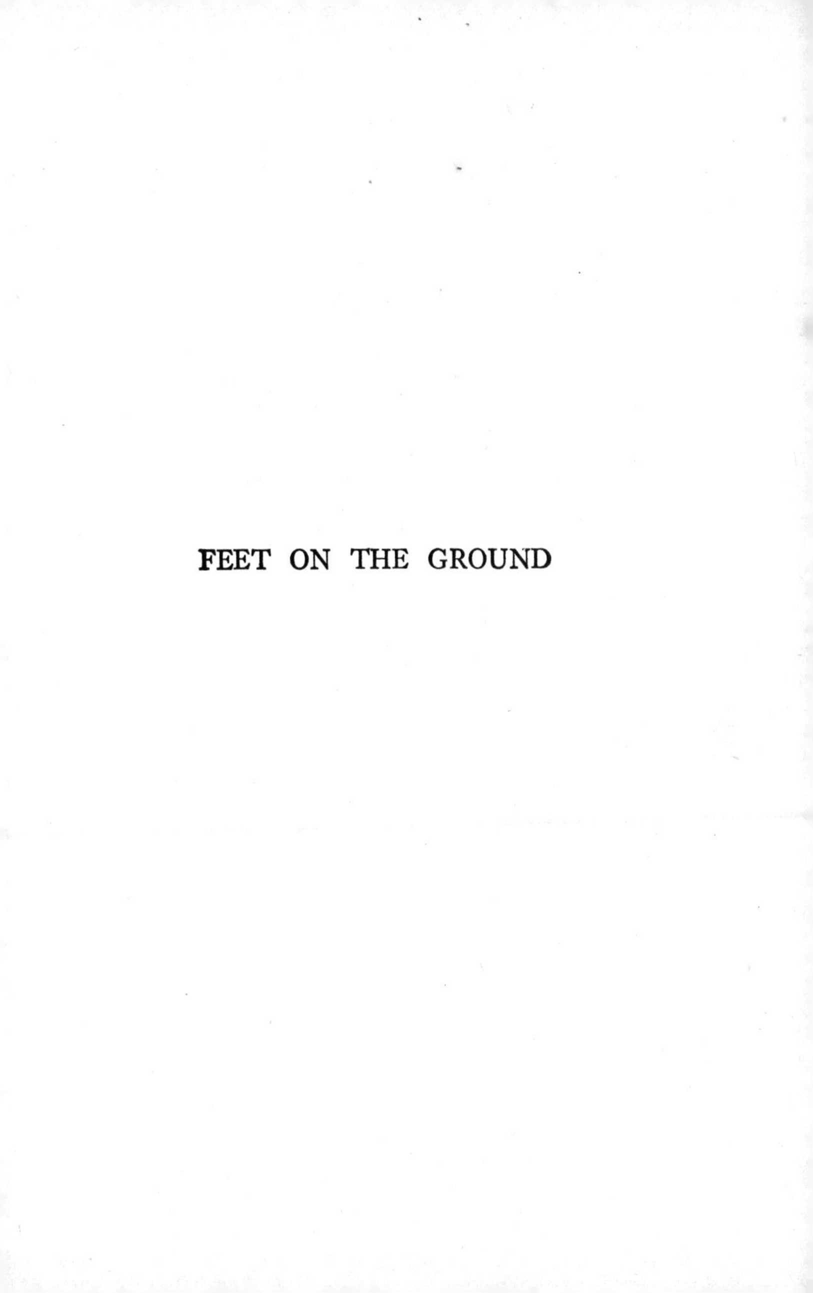

FEET ON THE GROUND

BLACKIE & SON LIMITED
16/18 William IV Street, Charing Cross, LONDON, W.C.2
17 Stanhope Street, GLASGOW

BLACKIE & SON (INDIA) LIMITED
103/5 Fort Street, BOMBAY

BLACKIE & SON (CANADA) LIMITED
TORONTO

FEET ON THE GROUND

being

An Approach to Modern Verse

by

MARGARET J. O'DONNELL, M.A.

Author of "An Anthology of Contemporary Verse" &c.

BLACKIE & SON LIMITED

LONDON AND GLASGOW

First printed 1940
Reprinted, with minor corrections, 1950
Reprinted 1950, 1951 (twice), 1952
Reprinted, with minor corrections 1953
Reprinted 1954

Printed in Great Britain by Blackie & Son, Ltd., Glasgow

To the Memory

of

My Father and Mother

FOREWORD

The approach to poetry outlined here, is in essence unpretentious, and that is why I have called the book *Feet on the Ground.* Although all the illustrations are drawn from modern verse, the approach is to poetry in general, and to modern verse only in so far as that represents a particular aspect of the general. I have made no attempt to search out examples of very recent verse, but on the contrary have deliberately chosen a great many that are widely known, so that the reader may relax from time to time in the company of the familiar.

Now that the book is written, I realize that the last word never can be said about the appeal of poetry. Analyse as we may, we still cannot explain why some poems move one to almost unbearable ecstasy. The last word, if it is ever said, will concern, not the poet—the giver, but the recipient—the reader. Without his inexplicable response to beauty, there is no Art.

CONTENTS

ACKNOWLEDGMENTS

The Editor and Publishers desire to make the following acknowledgments of permission to use Copyright poems in this volume.

The Author and Messrs. Victor Gollancz Ltd., for poem by L. Aaronson.

The Oxford University Press, for poems by L. Abercrombie and Gerard Manley Hopkins.

Messrs. Sidgwick & Jackson Ltd., for poems by J. Redwood Anderson and W. J. Turner.

Messrs. Martin Secker & Warburg Ltd., for poems by Martin Armstrong.

The Author, Messrs. Faber & Faber Ltd., and Random House, Inc., New York, for poems by W. H. Auden.

The Authors and Messrs. Gerald Duckworth & Co. Ltd., for poems by Hilaire Belloc, Osbert Sitwell, Edith Sitwell and Sacheverell Sitwell.

Mr. John Murray, for poem by John Betjeman.

Mr. Edmund Blunden.

The Author and Messrs. Constable & Co. Ltd.. for poem by Gordon Bottomley.

The Clarendon Press, Oxford, for poem *Cheddar Pinks* from "*New Verse*" by Robert Bridges, and four other poems from "*The Shorter Poems of Robert Bridges*".

Messrs. Sidgwick & Jackson Ltd. and Messrs. Dodd, Mead & Co., Inc., New York, for poem from "*The Collected Poems of Rupert Brooke*". (Copyright, 1915, by Dodd, Mead & Company.)

The Executrix of the late G. K. Chesterton and Messrs. Methuen & Co. Ltd., for poems by G. K. Chesterton from "*The Flying Inn*"; also reprinted by permission of Dodd, Mead & Company, Inc., New York.

Messrs. J. M. Dent & Sons Ltd., for poems by G. K. Chesterton and Richard Church.

The Author, Messrs. Macmillan & Co. Ltd., and The Macmillan Company, New York, for poems by Padraic Colum.

The Authors and Messrs. Jonathan Cape Ltd., for poems by W. H. Davies from "*Collected Poems*"; and poem by Stevie Smith from "*Tender Only to One*".

The Author, Messrs. Sidgwick & Jackson Ltd., and the Houghton Mifflin Company, Boston, for poem by John Drinkwater.

Messrs. Mathewson, Wilson & Smith, Montreal, for poem by Wm. H. Drummond.

The Author, Messrs. Faber & Faber Ltd., and Messrs. Harcourt, Brace & Co., Inc., New York, for four poems from "*Collected Poems of T. S. Eliot*" and two poems from "*Old Possum's Book of Practical Cats*", by T. S. Eliot.

Mrs. Flecker, Messrs. Martin Secker & Warburg Ltd., and Messrs. J. M. Dent & Sons Ltd., for poems from "*The Collected Poems of James Elroy Flecker*".

Messrs. Faber & Faber Ltd., for poem by J. Gould Fletcher.

The Author and Messrs. Constable & Co. Ltd., for poem by Dr. Robin Flower.

Messrs. Longmans Green & Co. Ltd., for poem by Stella Gibbons from "*The Mountain Beast*".

The Author, Messrs. Macmillan & Co. Ltd., and The Macmillan Company, New York, for poems by W. W. Gibson: *Breakfast* and *The Letter* from "*Collected Poems, 1905–1925*"; *Jungle Drums* from "*Islands*"; *The Release* from "*The Golden Room*" and "*Hazards*"; also the Oxford University Press for *The Match* from "*Coming and Going*".

Messrs. Wm. Heinemann Ltd., for poems by G. Rostrevor Hamilton and Arthur Symons.

Messrs Macmillan & Co. Ltd. and The Macmillan Company, New York, for poems from "*Collected Poems of Thomas Hardy*", by permission of the Trustees of the Hardy Estate.

Mr. F. W. Harvey.

The Author, Messrs. Macmillan & Co. Ltd., and The Macmillan Company, New York, for poems by Ralph Hodgson from "*Poems*".

Monsignor Ronald Knox.

Mrs. Frieda Lawrence, Messrs. Wm. Heinemann Ltd., and The Viking Press, Inc., New York, for poems from "*Collected Poems of D. H. Lawrence*".

The Hogarth Press, for poems by C. Day Lewis and F. L. Lucas.

The Author and the Houghton Mifflin Company, Boston, for poem by Amy Lowell.

The Author, Messrs. Faber & Faber Ltd., and Messrs. Henry Holt & Co., New York, for poems by Walter de la Mare.

Messrs. Faber & Faber Ltd. and Messrs. Doubleday, Doran & Co., Inc., New York, for poem from "archy & mehitabel" by Don Marquis. (Copyright, 1927, 1930 by Doubleday, Doran & Co., Inc.)

The Society of Authors (as Literary representative of Mr. John Masefield) and The Macmillan Company, New York, for poems by John Masefield.

Mrs. Monro and The Poetry Bookshop, for poems by Charlotte Mew and Harold Monro. Also Mrs. Monro, for extract from *To a Lady seen from the Train* by Frances Cornford in "*Spring Morning*".

The Author and the "*Boston Transcript*", for poem by Lilian Middleton.

Messrs. A. M. Heath & Co. Ltd., for poems by Edna St. Vincent Millay.

Mr. Seumas O'Sullivan.

Messrs. Chatto & Windus, for poems by Wilfred Owen.

The Author, Messrs. Faber & Faber Ltd., and Messrs. Harcourt Brace & Co., Inc., New York, for poem by Herbert Read from "*A World Within a War*".

The Hon. V. Sackville-West.

Messrs. Henry Holt & Co., New York, for poem by Carl Sandburg.

Mr. Siegfried Sassoon.

The Author and The Blythenhale Press, for poem by Stanley Snaith.

The Author and The Cambridge University Press, for poems by C. H. Sorley from "*Marlborough and Other Poems*".

Messrs. Faber & Faber Ltd. and The Random House, Inc., New York, for poem by Stephen Spender from "*Poems*"; and for poems by Louis MacNeice from "*The Earth Compels*" and "*Poems*".

Sir John C. Squire.

The Author, Messrs. Macmillan & Co. Ltd., and The Macmillan Company, New York, for poems by James Stephens from "*Collected Poems*" and "*Strict Joy 1931*".

Mr. L. A. G. Strong.

Mrs. Thomas and Messrs. Faber & Faber Ltd., for poems by Edward Thomas.

Mr. Edward Thompson.

Mr. Vyvyan Holland, for poem by Oscar Wilde.

Messrs. Basil Blackwell & Mott Ltd., Oxford, for poem by Humbert Wolfe.

Mrs. Yeats, Messrs. Macmillan & Co. Ltd., and The Macmillan Company, New York, for poems from "*The Collected Poems of W. B. Yeats*".

The Author and Messrs. W. Collins Sons & Co. Ltd., for poem by Francis Brett Young.

Mrs. Flecker, Messrs. Wm. Heinemann Ltd., and Messrs. Alfred A. Knopf, Inc., New York, for quotation from "*Hassan*" by James Elroy Flecker.

The Executors of the late Mary Webb, Messrs. Jonathan Cape Ltd., and Messrs. E. P. Dutton & Co., Inc., New York, for quotation from "*Robert Rideout's Pennillions*" in "*Seven for a Secret*" by Mary Webb.

The Editor and Publishers also wish to thank:—

Mr. Ronald Howie, for permission to quote from his unpublished poem *Hymn of Youth*.

Professor Gilbert Murray for permission to quote the passage on p. 5.

The Staff of the Cumberland Education Committee County Library for their co-operation.

CHAPTER ONE

"His Aim is Ecstasy"

NOTHING IS EASY!

Nothing is easy! Pity then
The poet more than other men.

And, since his aim is ecstasy,
And, since none work so hard as he,
Forgive the poet poesy!

He hath the same dull eyes: his ears
Are dull-attuned: his hopes and fears
Are those same ravening dogs that bay
The moon, and bury bones in clay!

Tho' he on offals, too, was bred,
Tho' in his heart, and in his head
The brute doth slaver, yet he can
Banish the brute from off the man,
The man from that beyond the man.

He gave a song, a wing, to words
That they might fly and sing like birds
In love, who cannot too much sing
The heaven, the earth, the everything;
And love, the air that buoys along
The wing, the singer, and the song.

Yea, wonder is that he hath done,
For all that is beneath the sun
By magic he transfigures to
A better sound, a finer view:
And—loveliest tale of all that's true!
He tells that you come to the spring,
And that the spring returns to you.

James Stephens.

The aim of this book is to shift the emphasis from the poet to the reader of poetry—from the craftsman to the consumer. Perhaps the poet will resent this, for like all artists he tends to repudiate his obligation to his readers, and the reader's rights over him. But just as a craftsman, unless he wants his work to find a permanent home only in a museum or a shop window, is dependent for his customers upon a public that appreciates his work, so a poet, unless he is concerned only with the writing and not at all with the permanence of his poetry, is dependent upon *his* customers—the people who read and accept his work. The verdict of posterity is the verdict of a discriminating poetry-reading public, not of a few contemporary critics and brother-poets. And therefore a poet who has at heart not only his own fame but the establishment of poetry as a universal art, should be very much concerned with educating a public taste, and spreading a wider knowledge of the technique and appreciation of poetry among ordinary people. So he should be prepared to concede that his poetry is not only the expression of his own emotion, but that it is also a means of communicating emotion and pleasure to the reader: he should allow the reader to put his own interpretation on the poet's creation; and even if he disagrees with this interpretation, he should rejoice to find that his poetry has more facets, more approaches, more interpretations than he discovered for himself. Shakespeare himself wrote better than he knew; and any poet may well be gratified if the most unlettered layman find in his poetry something—anything—to satisfy and please him.

In this book the reader is elevated above the poet inasmuch as it is *his* searchings and discoveries that are considered important, and the poetry (without regard to the poet) is the material found ready to his hand. And if he come to respect and love the poetry, shall he not also admire and worship the poet?

What is it that makes a poet? James Stephens, who ought to know, says that he is a man like other men, but with something in addition—the power to give wings to words. Stephens is too modest. The poet, like all artists, is something of a superman: his senses and feelings are super-acute; he has the power of seeing and hearing and feeling more sensitively than the rest of us. But extra sensitiveness to impressions is not all; he couples with it a craftsman's skill with words—he is able to make something memorable out of his experience.

How does a poem come into being? First the poet's feelings are aroused by some stimulus—it may be the first daffodils or the last rose; it may be the sound of rain on the roof or a symphony orchestra; it may be an idea, an enthusiasm of his own like the scorn of hypocrisy or love of the open air. Whatever the stimulus, the poet reacts to it, is inspired by it.

Sometimes the poem is written immediately; sometimes, long afterwards, the poet recalls the emotion he felt, and gives it expression. But seldom is a poem born without prolonged labour: first words are seldom the last, and the poet may change, recast and polish his verses for weeks, for months, sometimes for years.

Why does he do it? He does it because he must; because he has the divine gift of creation which cannot be denied: his heart grows hot within him and he must speak with his tongue.

Poets are not on the whole restful people to live with; the divine spark can grow into a fierce conflagration. For us, the homely glow of a strictly domestic fire—an *English* fire. For isn't there something alien, something foreign, about the passion and vehemence of poetry? Not in the least. And here is the paradox.

How would you describe the traditional Englishman? How does a foreigner describe him? As an uncultured, unintelligent, unimaginative, inarticulate player of games and maker of money. And yet the English people (and I do not mean British), have produced in the last four hundred years, the greatest poet and the finest body of lyrical poetry in the world. The English have a manifold genius, not least in the field of poetry. They are a nation of poets, though the individual Englishman is totally unaware of it and would heartily repudiate it.

I wonder why? For this gift of poetry is not something to be ashamed of. Indeed perhaps in it lies the secret of England's greatness, and we should do well to realize it. James Elroy Flecker, in his poetical drama " Hassan " says this:

" Ah! if there shall ever arise a nation whose people have forgotten poetry, or whose poets have forgotten the people, though they send their ships round Taprobane and their armies across the hills of Hindostan, though their city be greater than Babylon of old, though they mine a league into the earth or mount to the stars on wings—what of them? They will be a dark patch upon the world."

How can poetry be so important? It is because of the part it can play in deepening the wisdom and understanding and sympathy of men. Let Professor Gilbert Murray say it:

" Remember that in that inner world to which great literature belongs, a man may go on all his life learning to see, but he can never see all that is there; he can only hope to see deeper and deeper, more and more, and as he sees, to understand and to love."

Why is it then that this nation of poets does not on the whole make any attempt to look " deeper and deeper " into poetry, or " to understand and to love "? Possibly the cause lies away back in our schooldays. Teachers who make their own love and enthusiasm their only starting-point, invariably alienate all but the most sensitive of their pupils—

those who would probably become aware of poetry in any case. But the rest—the matter-of-fact, honest-to-goodness, football-playing, ragging, larking schoolboys, are made uncomfortable by a show of emotion, and so poetry becomes suspect. For these are young Englishmen, and they have all the Englishman's shyness and dread of emotional display.

Approach poetry therefore, reasonably and scientifically, and as awareness grows, emotion is born, but it is a controlled emotion, because its cause is understood. It is not a flood which drowns reason and drains away articulate speech, but a river flowing between sharply defined banks through a landscape clearly seen. Too many people still belong to the "Don't-brush-the-bloom-off-the-butterfly" school, and most of us are so filled with the idea that poetry must not be handled or examined too closely, that no wonder we are inarticulate about it. We cannot discuss something we are not allowed to see closely. Poets themselves are not without blame, for they have encouraged the idea that poetry is the concern of a chosen cultured few. To the ordinary man it is either a kind of Holy Grail, not to be looked upon, or something effeminate and totally unnecessary.

What is poetry then? It is an Art, like painting and music; and like all Arts it has a universal appeal because it appeals to the senses. But while there is nobody who does not like *some* kind of picture and *some* kind of music, there are a great many people who say they have no use for poetry.

Of all the Arts, music is most comparable with poetry, because it too appeals to the ear—it reaches our emotions primarily through the sense of hearing: poetry, like music, is intended to be heard. But here is where poetry has the advantage over music. Most of us are denied the pleasure of making music—that is of playing it or singing it—and we have to be content with listening to it, because we have never been taught to play or sing, or because we have no talent for it. But we all have a voice; we are capable of speech; the ability to read words comes to all of us in the ordinary course of our schooling; and " Allah made poetry a cheap thing to buy and a simple thing to understand ". So we can both listen to poetry, and speak it ourselves. It is the only Art in which one can become an executant without special talent and long training. In order to speak verse well enough to please ourselves, all we need is the verse. In order to speak it well enough to please other people, we need more, of course: an appreciation of rhythm, and sympathy with the poet's aim and emotion. But that is all. A big " all ", because it implies the ability to understand and appreciate what we read; but not an unattainable " all ", because there is no one who cannot learn how to study a poem so that even if he doesn't like it—if it doesn't appeal to him—if it isn't his kind of poetry—he can still appreciate and respect the craftsmanship, the skill that went to the making of it; and this respect and admiration for the sheer skill in the poet's handling of his material, is the first step towards appreciation of poetry.

Poetry is a virile Art—make no mistake about that. All kinds of men of action—soldiers, sailors, airmen, explorers, adventurers—have written poetry; because poetry is the most vigorous, the most concentrated, the most expressive kind of speech. And don't dismiss poetry as " sentimental ". It is true that a good deal of poetry is inspired by love, and by spring and birds and flowers; but it can deal with all kinds of other subjects too—everyday, homely, familiar, even sordid things: like railway trains, and aeroplanes, and ships, and gas and water mains, and pylons and gigantic cranes, and tenements with broken panes, and even—dare I say it? —drains! All the thousand and one things that excite or depress or thrill or enrage us, have the same effect on the poet; but he can put his feelings into words better than we can, and therefore we should respect this power that he has, the power to give " a song, a wing to words ", the magic by which he transfigures " all that is beneath the sun " to " a better sound, a finer view ".

Here are some examples of poetry expressing a powerful emotion. Three poets felt anger at the encroachment of the town and industry on the countryside, and all three of them express powerfully their anger and contempt, and their final satisfaction at the triumph of Nature over man-made things.

TO IRON-FOUNDERS AND OTHERS

When you destroy a blade of grass
  You poison England at her roots:
Remember no man's foot can pass
  Where evermore no green life shoots.

You force the birds to wing too high
  Where your unnatural vapours creep:
Surely the living rocks shall die
  When birds no rightful distance keep.

You have brought down the firmament
  And yet no heaven is more near;
You shape huge deeds without event,
  And half-made men believe and fear.

Your worship is your furnaces,
  Which, like old idols, lost obscenes,
Have molten bowels; your vision is
  Machines for making more machines.

O, you are busied in the night
  Preparing destinies of rust;
Iron misused must turn to blight
  And dwindle to a tettered crust.

The grass, forerunner of life, has gone,
  But plants that spring in ruins and shards
Attend until your dream is done:
  I have seen hemlock in your yards.

The generations of the worm
  Know not your loads piled on their soil;
Their knotted ganglions shall wax firm
  Till your strong flag-stones heave and toil.

When the old hollowed earth is cracked,
  And when, to grasp more power and feasts,
Its ores are emptied, wasted, lacked,
  The middens of your burning beasts

Shall be raked over till they yield
  Last priceless slags for fashionings high,
Ploughs to make grass in every field,
  Chisels men's hands to magnify.

Gordon Bottomley.

TO SOME BUILDERS OF CITIES

You have thrust Nature out, to make
A wilderness where nothing grows
But forests of unbudding stone
(The sparrow's lonely for his boughs);
You fling up citadels to stay
The soft invasion of the rose.

But though you put the Earth in thrall
And ransack all her fragrant dowers,
Her old accomplice, Heaven, will plot
To take with stars your roofs and towers;
And neither stone nor steel can foil
That silver strategy of flowers.

Stanley Snaith.

BELEAGUERED CITIES

Build your houses, build your houses, build your
towns,
Fell the woodland, to a gutter turn the brook,
Pave the meadows, pave the meadows, pave the downs,
Plant your bricks and mortar where the grasses shook,
The wind-swept grasses shook.
Build, build your Babels black against the sky—
But mark yon small green blade, your stones between,
The single spy
Of that uncounted host you have outcast;
For with their tiny pennons waving green
They shall storm your streets at last.

Build your houses, build your houses, build your slums,
Drive your drains where once the rabbits used to lurk,
Let there be no song there save the wind that hums
Through the idle wires while dumb men tramp to
work,
Tramp to their idle work.
Silent the siege; none notes it; yet one day
Men from your walls shall watch the woods once more
Close round their prey.
Build, build the ramparts of your giant-town;
Yet they shall crumble to the dust before
The battering thistle-down.

F. L. Lucas.

Did you notice, by the way, how effectively F. L. Lucas makes use of the consonant " b "? It is a most satisfying sound, full of barely suppressed violence. (That is why so many expletives begin with it, of course—like " Bother "!) Lucas gets all the necessary effect with:

> Build, build your Babels black against the sky.

Notice, too, the use of military metaphors in two of the poems:

> But mark yon small green blade, your stones between,
> The single spy
> Of that uncounted host you have outcast;
> For with their tiny pennons waving green
> They shall storm your streets at last.

And:

> Silent the siege; none notes it; yet one day
> Men from your walls shall watch the woods once more
> Close round their prey.

And, with a specially effective paradox in the last line:

> Build, build the ramparts of your giant-town;
> Yet they shall crumble to the dust before
> The battering thistle-down.

In Snaith's poem too:

> You fling up citadels to stay
> The soft invasion of the rose.
>
> But though you put the Earth in thrall
> And ransack all her fragrant dowers,
> Her old accomplice, Heaven, will plot
> To take with stars your roofs and towers;
> And neither stone nor steel can foil
> That silver strategy of flowers.

Those are three examples of powerful poetry. Poetry must be powerful enough to stimulate, to excite, to move and to satisfy us, by saying for us what we cannot say ourselves. We may like towns; we may disagree with these three poets; but we must admit that they can express their feelings with a power denied to us.

James Stephens says: " Pity the poet "; but Charles Hamilton Sorley says more truly: " Pity us who are not poets, because we suffer too, but in silence; we love but we cannot speak; we are workers but not creators; we have ' the bitter agony ' but are denied the relief of ' the bitter cry '."

TO POETS

We are the homeless, even as you,
Who hope and never can begin.
Our hearts are wounded through and through
Like yours, but our hearts bleed within.
We too make music, but our tones
'Scape not the barrier of our bones.

We have no comeliness like you.
We toil, unlovely, and we spin.
We start, return: we wind, undo:
We hope, we err, we strive, we sin,
We love: your love's not greater, but
The lips of our loves might stay shut.

We have the evil spirits too
That shake our soul with battle-din.
But we have an eviller spirit than you,
We have a dumb spirit within:
The exceeding bitter agony
But not the exceeding bitter cry.

Charles Hamilton Sorley

CHAPTER TWO

You *Can* Brush the Bloom off a Butterfly

BALLADE OF THE POETIC LIFE

The fat men go about the streets,
The politicians play their game,
The prudent bishops sound retreats,
And think the martyrs much to blame;
Honour and love are halt and lame
And Greed and Power are deified,
The wild are harnessed by the tame;
For this the poets lived and died.

Shelley's a trademark used on sheets.
Aloft the sky in words of flame
We read " What porridge had John Keats?
Why Brown's! A hundred years the same!"
Arcadia's an umbrella frame,
Milton's a toothpaste; from the tide
Sappho's been dredged to rouge my Dame—
For this the poets lived and died.

And yet, to launch ideal fleets
Lost regions in the stars to claim,
To face all ruins and defeats,
To sing a beaten world to shame,

To hold each bright impossible aim
Deep in the heart; to starve in pride
For fame, and never know their fame—
For this the poets lived and died.

ENVOI

Princess, inscribe beneath my name
" He never begged, he never sighed,
He took his medicine as it came "—
For this the poets lived—and died.

Sir John Squire.

Those people who say they have no use for poetry, really mean, I expect, that they would never dream of drawing their chairs up to the fire and settling down to a comfortable evening with a book of verse instead of a good detective novel. Well, of course not. I'm sure there are very few people who choose poetry as their favourite kind of recreational reading. Poetry is an Art, to be enjoyed when you are in the mood for it. It is not a substitute for, nor is it in the same category with reading for relaxation, because it does not let you relax: it stirs you. But some poetry can be enjoyed without any effort at all. What about this, by that jovial lover of good ale, G. K. Chesterton? Read it aloud with a good swinging rhythm, rolling the " r's " and giving full value to the consonant sounds.

THE ROLLING ENGLISH ROAD

Before the Roman came to Rye or out to Severn strode,
The rolling English drunkard made the rolling English
road.
A reeling road, a rolling road, that rambles round the
shire,
And after him the parson ran, the sexton and the squire;
A merry road, a mazy road, and such as we did tread
The night we went to Birmingham by way of Beachy
Head.

I knew no harm of Bonaparte and plenty of the Squire,
And for to fight the Frenchman I did not much desire;
But I did bash their baggonets because they came
arrayed
To straighten out the crooked road an English drunkard
made,
Where you and I went down the lane with ale-mugs in
our hands,
The night we went to Glastonbury by way of Goodwin
Sands.

His sins they were forgiven him; or why do flowers run
Behind him; and the hedges all strengthening in the
sun?
The wild thing went from left to right and knew not
which was which,
But the wild rose was above him when they found him
in the ditch.
God pardon us, nor harden us; we did not see so clear
The night we went to Bannockburn by way of Brighton
Pier.

My friends, we will not go again or ape an ancient rage,
Or stretch the folly of our youth to be the shame of age,
But walk with clearer eyes and ears this path that
wandereth,
And see undrugged in evening light the decent inn of
death;
For there is good news yet to hear and fine things to be
seen,
Before we go to Paradise by way of Kensal Green.

G. K. Chesterton.

Did you like that? Well, that is poetry, you know. So is this: " Tarantella " by Hilaire Belloc. It is another good swinging poem, easy to listen to. Read it aloud, leaning on the rhymes and not forgetting the internal ones.

TARANTELLA

Do you remember an Inn,
Miranda?
Do you remember an Inn?
And the tedding and the spreading
Of the straw for a bedding,
And the fleas that tease in the High Pyrenees,
And the wine that tasted of the tar?
And the cheers and the jeers of the young muleteers
(Under the vine of the dark verandah)?
Do you remember an Inn, Miranda,
Do you remember an Inn?
And the cheers and the jeers of the young muleteers
Who hadn't got a penny,

And who weren't paying any,
And the hammer at the doors and the Din?
And the Hip! Hop! Hap!
Of the clap
Of the hands to the twirl and the swirl
Of the girl gone chancing,
Glancing,
Dancing,
Backing and advancing,
Snapping of the clapper to the spin
Out and in—
And the Ting, Tong, Tang of the guitar!
Do you remember an Inn,
Miranda,
Do you remember an Inn?

Never more,
Miranda,
Never more.
Only the high peaks hoar:
And Aragon a torrent at the door.
No sound
In the walls of the Halls where falls
The tread
Of the feet of the dead to the ground.
No sound:
But the boom
Of the far Waterfall like Doom.

Hilaire Belloc.

Here is a poem by Martin Armstrong, about a pathetic, lonely old spinster out for a day's shopping:

MISS THOMPSON GOES SHOPPING

MISS THOMPSON AT HOME.

In her lone cottage on the downs,
With winds and blizzards and great crowns
Of shining cloud, with wheeling plover
And short grass sweet with the small white
    clover,
Miss Thompson lived, correct and meek,
A lonely spinster, and every week
On market-day she used to go
Into the little town below,
Tucked into the great downs' hollow bowl
Like pebbles gathered in a shoal.

SHE GOES A-MARKETING.

So, having washed her plates and cup
And banked the kitchen-fire up,
Miss Thompson slipped upstairs and
    dressed,
Put on her black (her second best),
The bonnet trimmed with rusty plush,
Peeped in the glass with simpering blush,
From camphor-smelling cupboard took
Her thicker jacket off the hook
Because the day might turn to cold.
Then, ready, slipped downstairs and rolled
The hearthrug back; then searched about,
Found her basket, ventured out,
Snecked the door and paused to lock it
And plunge the key in some deep pocket.
Then as she tripped demurely down
The steep descent, the little town
Spread wider till its sprawling street
Enclosed her and her footfalls beat
On hard stone pavement, and she felt
Those throbbing ecstasies that melt

Through heart and mind, as happy, free,
Her small, prim personality
Merged into the seething strife
Of auction-marts and city life.

SHE VISITS THE BOOT-MAKER.

Serenely down the busy stream
Miss Thompson floated in a dream.
Now, hovering bee-like, she would stop
Entranced before some tempting shop,
Getting in people's way and prying
At things she never thought of buying:
Now wafted on without an aim,
Until in course of time she came
To Watson's bootshop. Long she pries
At boots and shoes of every size—
Brown football-boots with bar and stud
For boys that scuffle in the mud,
And dancing-pumps with pointed toes,
Glossy as jet, and dull black bows;
Slim ladies' shoes with two-inch heel
And sprinkled beads of gold and steel—
" How any one can wear such things!"
On either side the doorway springs
(As in a tropic jungle loom
Masses of strange thick-petalled bloom
And fruits mis-shapen) fold on fold
A growth of sand-shoes, rubber-soled,
Clambering the door-posts, branching, spawning
Their barbarous bunches like an awning
Over the windows and the doors.
But, framed among the other stores,
Something has caught Miss Thompson's eye
(O worldliness; O vanity!)
A pair of slippers—scarlet plush.

Miss Thompson feels a conscious blush
Suffuse her face, as though her thought
Had ventured further than it ought.
But O that colour's rapturous singing
And the answer in her lone heart ringing!
She turns (O Guardian Angels stop her
From doing anything improper!)
She turns; and see, she stoops and bungles
In through the sand-shoes' hanging jungles,
Away from light and common sense,
Into the shop dim-lit and dense
With smells of polish and tanned hide.

MRS. WATSON.

Soon from a dark recess inside
Fat Mrs. Watson comes slip-slop
To mind the business of the shop.
She walks flat-footed with a roll—
A serviceable, homely soul,
With kindly, ugly face like dough,
Hair dull and colourless as tow.
A huge Scotch pebble fills the space
Between her bosom and her face.
One sees her making beds all day.
Miss Thompson lets her say her say:
" So chilly for the time of year.
It's ages since we saw you here."
Then, heart a-flutter, speech precise,
Describes the shoes and asks the price.
" Them, Miss? Ah them is six-and-nine."
Miss Thompson shudders down the spine
(Dreams of impossible romance).

WRESTLES WITH A TEMPTATION;

She eyes them with a wistful glance,
Torn between good and evil. Yes,
For half-a-minute and no less
Miss Thompson strives with seven devils,

AND IS SAVED.

Then, soaring over earthly levels,
Turns from the shoes with lingering touch—
" Ah, six-and-nine is far too much.
Sorry to trouble you. Good-day!"

SHE VISITS THE FISH-MONGER.

A little farther down the way
Stands Miles's fish-shop, whence is shed
So strong a smell of fishes dead
That people of a subtler sense
Hold their breath and hurry thence.
Miss Thompson hovers there and gazes:
Her housewife's knowing eye appraises
Salt and fresh, severely cons
Kippers bright as tarnished bronze:
Great cods disposed upon the sill,
Chilly and wet, with gaping gill,
Flat head, glazed eye, and mute, uncouth,
Shapeless, wan, old-woman's mouth.
Next a row of soles and plaice
With querulous and twisted face,
And red-eyed bloaters, golden-grey;
Smoked haddocks ranked in neat array;
A group of smelts that take the light
Like slips of rainbow, pearly bright;
Silver trout with rosy spots,
And coral shrimps with keen black dots
For eyes, and hard and jointed sheath
And crisp tails curving underneath.
But there upon the sanded floor,
More wonderful in all that store
Than anything on slab or shelf,

MR. MILES.

Stood Miles, the fishmonger, himself.
Four-square he stood and filled the place.
His huge hands and his jolly face
Were red. He had a mouth to quaff

Pint after pint; a sounding laugh,
But wheezy at the end, and oft
His eyes bulged outwards and he coughed.
Aproned he stood from chin to toe,
The apron's vertical long flow
Warped grandly outwards to display
His hale round belly hung midway,
Whose apex was securely bound
With apron-strings wrapped round and
round.
Outside, Miss Thompson, small and staid,
Felt, as she always felt, afraid
Of this huge man who laughed so loud
And drew the notice of the crowd.
Awhile she paused in timid thought,
Then promptly hurried in and bought
" Two kippers, please. Yes, lovely weather."
" Two kippers? Sixpence altogether."
And in the basket laid the pair
Wrapped face to face in newspaper.

RELAPSES INTO TEMPTATION. AND FALLS.

Then on she went, as one half blind,
For things were stirring in her mind;
Then turned about with fixed intent
And, heading for the bootshop, went
Straight in and bought the scarlet slippers
And popped them in beside the kippers.

SHE VISITS THE CHEMIST.

So much for that. From there she tacked,
Still flushed by this decisive act,
Westward, and came without a stop
To Mr. Wren the chemist's shop,
And stood awhile outside to see
The tall, big-bellied bottles three—
Red, blue, and emerald, richly bright

Each with its burning core of light.
The bell chimed as she pushed the door.
Spotless the oilcloth on the floor,
Limpid as water each glass case,
Each thing precisely in its place.
Rows of small drawers, black-lettered each
With curious words of foreign speech,
Ranked high above the other ware.
The old strange fragrance filled the air,
A fragrance like the garden pink,
But tinged with vague medicinal stink
Of camphor, soap, new sponges, blent
With chloroform and violet scent.

MR. WREN.

And Wren the chemist, tall and spare,
Stood gaunt behind his counter there.
Quiet and very wise he seemed,
With skull-like face, bald head that gleamed;
Through spectacles his eyes looked kind.
He wore a pencil tucked behind
His ear. And never he mistakes
The wildest signs the doctor makes
Prescribing drugs. Brown paper, string,
He will not use for any thing,
But all in neat white parcels packs
And sticks them up with sealing-wax.
Miss Thompson bowed and blushed, and
then
Undoubting bought of Mr. Wren,
Being free from modern scepticism,
A bottle for her rheumatism;
Also some peppermints to take
In case of wind; an oval cake
Of scented soap; a penny square
Of pungent naphthaline to scare

The moth. And after Wren had wrapped
And sealed the lot, Miss Thompson clapped
Them in beside the fish and shoes;
" Good-day," she says, and off she goes.

IS LED AWAY TO THE PLEASURES OF THE TOWN. SUCH AS GROCERIES AND MILLINERY,

Beelike, Miss Thompson, whither next?
Outside, you pause awhile, perplext,
Your bearings lost. Then all comes back,
And round she wheels, hot on the track
Of Giles the grocer, and from there
To Emilie the milliner,
There to be tempted by the sight
Of hats and blouses fiercely bright.
(O guard Miss Thompson, Powers that Be,
From Crudeness and Vulgarity.)

AND OTHER ALLUREMENTS.

Still on from shop to shop she goes
With sharp bird's-eye, inquiring nose,
Prying and peering, entering some,
Oblivious of the thought of home.
The town brimmed up with deep-blue haze,
But still she stayed to flit and gaze,
Her eyes ablur with rapturous sights,
Her small soul full of small delights,
Empty her purse, her basket filled.

BUT AT LENGTH IS CONVINCED OF INDISCRETION.

The traffic in the town was stilled.
The clock struck six. Men thronged the inns.
Dear, dear, she should be home long since.

AND RETURNS HOME.

Then as she climbed the misty downs
The lamps were lighted in the town's
Small streets. She saw them star by star
Multiplying from afar;

Till, mapped beneath her, she could trace
Each street, and the wide square market-
place
Sunk deeper and deeper as she went
Higher up the steep ascent.
And all that soul-uplifting stir
Step by step fell back from her,
The glory gone, the blossoming
Shrivelled, and she, a small frail thing,
Carrying her laden basket. Till
Darkness and silence of the hill
Received her in their restful care
And stars came dropping through the air.

But loudly, sweetly sang the slippers
In the basket with the kippers;
And loud and sweet the answering thrills
From her lone heart on the hills.

Martin Armstrong.

Confess it now. There's something about poetry that affects you. What is it? Well, the obvious thing is the grand swing that it has, the rhythm of it. The words are arranged so that the stresses fall regularly, whereas in ordinary speech they come haphazard. We all respond to rhythm: soldiers march better with a band than without one; the rhythm of the dance-music sets our feet dancing in time to it; we walk and breathe rhythmically. Another obvious attraction is the rhyme, that pleasing echo of sound that comes naturally to us. Don't forget that—it *is* a natural device, for don't we all rhyme instinctively in baby-talk? Rhyme and rhythm are both so attractive that we remember much more easily, phrases and sayings that have one or both. Look at our proverbs: " A stitch in time saves nine "; " Birds of a feather flock together "; and how attractive and memorable are the nursery rhyme jingles: " Jack and Jill went up the hill "; and " Old Mother Hubbard went to the cupboard ". Yes, rhyme and rhythm are, both of them, attractive and natural, and when the poet deliberately abandons either, he has to put in something else to make up for the lack—his lines must have an extra power and music.

These are two of the things that make verse more attractive than prose: in fact they constitute the whole difference between prose and verse, broadly speaking. Of course, all verse is not rhymed (blank verse for instance), and not all verse has regular rhythm; but most verse has. Here are two passages that illustrate the difference between prose and verse:

TUGS

" At midday the tugs gliding down the river, followed by strings of barges, have a certain dignity; but at night, black against the sky, and lit up only by the red and green of their port and starboard lamps, they have an air of glamour and romance."

TUGS

At noon three English dowagers ride
Stiff of neck and dignified,
Margaret, *Maud* and *Mary Blake*,
With servile barges in their wake:

But silhouetted at midnight,
Darkly, by green and crimson light,
Three Nubian queens pass down the Thames
Statelily with flashing gems.

G. Rostrevor Hamilton.

There are other differences between those two passages, besides the fact that one is written in prose while the other has both rhythm and rhyme; the poem contains vivid description and imaginative power, qualities which we shall discuss later.

And now, quite apart from whether you like poetry or not, don't you think it worth while to become a critical judge of at least this one Art, to be able to recognize one poem as good, and reject another as mere verse? You can, you know. By practice in examining and analysing, you do arrive at the stage when you know a good poem from a bad one. In the untrained, intuition and feeling are unreliable guides; something much more scientific is needed. However exquisitely beautiful a poem may be, it can stand up to any amount of man-handling. It is not a delicate piece of pottery that clumsy hands may drop and break in pieces. It can be analysed, dissected, put under the microscope; and the closer and more detailed the examination, the more one finds to admire, as with any work of art. A poem is not a butterfly, which when dis-sected is very, very dead, and very little like a butterfly. The poem is a poem still, appreciated all the more because close and detailed examination have discovered to the student, beauties and skill which were not obvious at first. You cannot brush the bloom off a poem; analysis cannot kill it, any more than the use of poets' names as trade-marks can dim their glory or prostitute their fame, in spite of Sir John Squire's satirical little " Ballade " with which this chapter opened.

Perhaps you still think you don't like poetry. But if by study and analysis you find that the poet has done something that you cannot do, then you may begin to respect him, and that is the first step towards appreciation in any Art.

Start off with your feet fixed firmly on the ground, and examine and analyse the poem coldly and scientifically, and sooner—or later—your feelings will take charge, and you will find yourself air-borne, whirled aloft on the " viewless wings of Poesy ". O yes, you will!

CHAPTER THREE

Feet on the Ground

ANY LITTLE OLD SONG

Any little old song
  Will do for me,
Tell it of joys long gone,
  Or joys to be,
Or friendly faces best
  Loved to see.

Newest themes I want not
  On subtle strings,
And for thrillings pant not
  That new song brings:
I only need the homeliest
  Of heart-stirrings.

Thomas Hardy.

Poetry was originally intended to be heard—to be recited or sung, and its first appeal therefore, is to the ear. An understanding of the sense is not essential for appreciation of the sound: the rhythm, music and mood can be felt and enjoyed even if the poem is in a foreign language of which not one word can be understood. This, however, is only partial appreciation; understanding of the subject matter is necessary for full enjoyment. We must be prepared then, to spend some time and thought on studying a poem, and our first concern shall be with the subject. Now, with feet firmly fixed on the ground, we are ready to take the first step. We must read the poem once, twice, perhaps even three times, listening to the sounds, and feeling the swing of it. There is no need to speak the verse aloud. It is possible, by reading the poem silently, at a speaking pace, not with the eye alone, but shaping the sounds and being aware of them with the ear of the mind, to " hear " the poem sometimes more satisfactorily than if we were to speak it aloud.

Then we must find out what the poem is about. The title helps of course, but that is not enough. We must find out what was the poet's intention and aim in writing it; what gave him his inspiration; what impelled him to write; what aspect of the subject he is concerned with. This poem for instance—" The Quails " by Francis Brett Young—is it enough to say that it is about quails? The first four lines tell us what aspect of the subject the poet is dealing with: the trapping of quails by means of a decoy. But is that the whole subject? Read the poem and see what you think.

THE QUAILS

(In the south of Italy the peasants put out the eyes of a captured quail so that its cries may attract the flocks of spring migrants into their nets.)

All through the night
I have heard the stuttering call of a blind quail,
A caged decoy, under a cairn of stones,
Crying for light as the quails cry for love.

Other wanderers,
Northward from Africa winging on numb pinions, dazed
With beating winds and the sobbing of the sea,
Hear, in a breath of sweet land-herbage, the call
Of the blind one, their sister . . .
Hearing, their fluttered hearts
Take courage, and they wheel in their dark flight,
Knowing that their toil is over, dreaming to see
The white stubbles of Abruzzi smitten with dawn,
And spilt grain lying in the furrows, the squandered gold
That is the delight of quails in their spring mating.

Land-scents grow keener,
Penetrating the dank and bitter odour of brine
That whitens their feathers;
Far below, the voice of their sister calls them
To plenty, and sweet water, and fulfilment.
Over the pallid margin of dim seas breaking,
Over the thickening in the darkness that is land,
They fly. Their flight is ended. Wings beat no more,

Downward they drift, one by one, like dark petals,
Slowly, listlessly falling
Into the mouth of horror:
The nets . . .
Where men come trampling and crying with bright lanterns,
Plucking their weak, entangled claws from the meshes of net,
Clutching the soft brown bodies mottled with olive,
Crushing the warm, fluttering flesh, in hands stained with blood,
Till their quivering hearts are stilled, and the bright eyes
That are like a polished agate, glaze in death.

But the blind one, in her wicker cage, without ceasing
Haunts this night of spring with her stuttering call,
Knowing nothing of the terror that walks in darkness,
Knowing only that some cruelty has stolen the light
That is life, and that she must cry until she dies.

I, in the darkness,
Heard, and my heart grew sick. But I know that to-morrow
A smiling peasant will come with a basket of quails
Wrapped in vine-leaves, prodding them with blood-stained fingers,
Saying, " Signore, you must cook them thus, and thus,
With a sprig of basil inside them." And I shall thank him,
Carrying the piteous carcases into the kitchen
Without a pang, without shame.

" Why should I be ashamed? Why should I rail
Against the cruelty of men? Why should I pity,

Seeing that there is no cruelty which men can imagine
To match the subtle dooms that are wrought against
them
By blind spores of pestilence: seeing that each of us,
Lured by dim hopes, flutters in the toils of death
On a cold star that is spinning blindly through space
Into the nets of time?"

So cried I, bitterly thrusting pity aside,
Closing my lids to sleep. But sleep came not,
And pity, with sad eyes,
Crept to my side, and told me
That the life of all creatures is brave and pityful
Whether they be men, with dark thoughts to vex them,
Or birds, wheeling in the swift joys of flight,
Or brittle ephemerids, spinning to death in the haze
Of gold that quivers on dim evening waters;
Nor would she be denied.
The harshness died
Within me, and my heart
Was caught and fluttered like the palpitant heart
Of a brown quail, flying
To the call of her blind sister
And death, in the spring night.

Francis Brett Young.

It is not enough, is it, to say that the subject of this poem is the catching of quails? No; the poet is concerned, not with describing that process to us, but with analysing his own reactions to the cry of the blinded quail in the night. He hears it; he knows what it is; his imagination too vividly pictures the scene, and his emotions are stirred so that he cannot sleep for pity. He knows nevertheless that, next day, he will buy and eat the quails that are brought to his door—and will enjoy them; and he despises himself for his insensitiveness. Then he tries to justify himself: after all, why call men cruel when creatures in the natural course of their lives are made to suffer more cruelly still from diseases that afflict them; when men themselves are victims of death and suffering? . . . But reason cannot quench emotion; pity will not be banished; and the poet lies sleepless, sharing all the sufferings of all creatures, in an anguish of compassion.

That is what the poem is about: the emotion aroused in the poet by an external stimulus. The poet is not alone in his response to such stimuli, for all of us respond in varying degrees to what we observe around us; but the poet is more acute in his observation, more sensitive to impressions, more passionately moved than we ordinary people are.

Poetry, like all creative art, is born of emotional stress and is brought forth in labour. The poem delivered, its author finds relief, and spiritual and mental peace. Thus it is that poetry has a healing influence not only on the poet, but on the reader, who, inarticulate himself, finds in another's expression the remedy for his own sickness. So, when we come to study the subject matter of a poem, we cannot separate from it the poet's emotion; and although for convenience' sake we are considering "Mood and Emotion" as our second step in appreciation, we must remember that the road we are going along, does not consist of a series of "steps", but that it is a gradual slope, one "step" merging almost insensibly into the next. Consideration of subject, for instance, sometimes overlaps another " step " which we shall label Imagery. Poetry does not always mean exactly what it says. The poet uses figures of speech, and clothes his thought in figurative language, which must be interpreted and given a literal translation. Here, for instance, is a lovely poem by Walter de la Mare:

NOD

Softly along the road of evening,
  In a twilight dim with rose,
Wrinkled with age, and drenched with dew
  Old Nod, the shepherd, goes.

His drowsy flock streams on before him,
  Their fleeces charged with gold,
To where the sun's last beam leans low
  On Nod the shepherd's fold.

The hedge is quick and green with briar,
  From their sand the conies creep;
And all the birds that fly in heaven
  Flock singing home to sleep.

His lambs outnumber a noon's roses,
  Yet, when night's shadows fall,
His blind old sheep-dog, Slumber-soon,
  Misses not one of all.

His are the quiet steeps of dreamland,
  The waters of no-more-pain,
His ram's bell rings 'neath an arch of stars,
  " Rest, rest, and rest again."

Walter de la Mare.

What would you say is the subject? An old man and his sheep-dog? No, of course not: it is about sleep. The figure of speech used is Personification, for sleep is represented as a person.

Here is another poem:

THE SNARE

I hear a sudden cry of pain!
  There is a rabbit in a snare:
Now I hear the cry again,
  But I cannot tell from where.

But I cannot tell from where
  He is calling out for aid;
Crying on the frightened air,
  Making everything afraid.

Making everything afraid,
  Wrinkling up his little face,
As he cries again for aid;
  And I cannot find the place!

And I cannot find the place
  Where his paw is in the snare:
Little one! Oh, little one!
  I am searching everywhere.

James Stephens.

There is nothing figurative about that—it really is about a rabbit caught in a snare.

One poet writing about a rose, really does mean "the last rose of summer"; but Yeats means something quite different:

TO THE ROSE UPON THE ROOD OF TIME

Red Rose, proud Rose, sad Rose of all my days!
Come near me, while I sing the ancient ways:
Cuchulain battling with the bitter tide;
The Druid, grey, wood-nurtured, quiet-eyed,
Who cast round Fergus dreams, and ruin untold;
And thine own sadness, whereof stars, grown old
In dancing silver sandalled on the sea,
Sing in their high and lonely melody.
Come near, that no more blinded by man's fate,
I find under the boughs of love and hate,
In all poor foolish things that live a day,
Eternal beauty wandering on her way.

Come near, come near, come near—Ah, leave me still
A little space for the rose-breath to fill!
Lest I no more hear common things that crave;
The weak worm hiding down in its small cave,
The field mouse running by me in the grass,
And heavy mortal hopes that toil and pass;
But seek alone to hear the strange things said
By God to the bright hearts of those long dead,
And learn to chaunt a tongue men do not know.
Come near; I would, before my time to go,
Sing of old Eire, and the ancient ways:
Red Rose, proud Rose, sad Rose of all my days.

William Butler Yeats.

Any subject capable of inspiring emotion, is suitable for poetry; but as some subjects more than others have always aroused deep feeling, it is not surprising to find that the bulk of our English lyric poetry is concerned with them: love, nature, religion, patriotism, the sea, life and death. These persist in spite of movements which have arisen from time to time in the history of English poetry to bring subjects more in touch with contemporary life, and violent controversies have arisen on the suitability of new subjects. In our own time, a similar movement is under way, and in addition to the universal themes referred to, you will find in any anthology of modern verse, poems on steam-engines, electricity pylons, cement-mixers, factories, aeroplanes—all subjects which are familiar and therefore attractive to us, because they are part and parcel of the life we live. Here are two of them:

THE PIGEON

Throb, throb from the mixer
Spewing out concrete.
And at the heads of the cables
Stand the serpent-warders,
Sweating and straining,
Thrusting those cruel mouths to their prey.

Hark how the steel tongues hiss
As they stab.
The men sway under the effort,
And their eyes are bloodshot with the din,
The clatter that shatters the brain.
Throb, throb from the mixer
Spewing out concrete.

The crowd stands by
Watching the smoothers;
Fascinated by the flat, wet levels
Of newlaid cement.
See how those curdled lakes
Glisten under the sky,
Virginal.

Then the dusty air suddenly divides,
And a pigeon from a plane-tree
Flutters down to bathe its wings in that
mirage of water.
But deceived, and angry,
Bewildered by the din,
The throb, throb from the mixer
Spewing out concrete,
It backs upon its wing,
Threshes air, and is gone.

But there, in the deflowered bed,
Is the seal of its coral foot,
Set till rocks crumble.

Richard Church.

MORNING EXPRESS

Along the wind-swept platform, pinched and white,
The travellers stand in pools of wintry light,
Offering themselves to morn's long, slanting arrows.
The train's due; porters trundle laden barrows.
The train steams in, volleying resplendent clouds
Of sun-blown vapour. Hither and about,
Scared people hurry, storming the doors in crowds.
The officials seem to waken with a shout,

Resolved to hoist and plunder; some to the vans
Leap; others rumble the milk in gleaming cans.

Boys, indolent-eyed, from baskets leaning back,
Question each face; a man with a hammer steals
Stooping from coach to coach; with clang and clack,
Touches and tests, and listens to the wheels.
Guard sounds a warning whistle, points to the clock
With brandished flag, and on his folded flock
Claps the last door: the monster grunts: "Enough!"
Tightening his load of links with pant and puff.
Under the arch, then forth into blue day,
Glide the processional windows on their way,
And glimpse the stately folk who sit at ease
To view the world like kings taking the seas
In prosperous weather: drifting banners tell
Their progress to the counties; with them goes
The clamour of their journeying; while those
Who sped them stand to wave a last farewell.

Siegfried Sassoon.

The "country house" as a feature of English life, is disappearing with the leisure and the wealth that made it possible. Its place has been taken by the week-end cottage, as delightful an institution as the national habit of "week-ending", that symbol of freedom from the constraints and demands of our working-day lives. A poem about a week-end cottage is bound to have an instantaneous appeal:

WEEK-END

I

The train! The twelve o'clock for paradise,
  Hurry, or it will try to creep away.
Out in the country everyone is wise:
  We can be only wise on Saturday.
There you are waiting, little friendly house:
  Those are your chimney-stacks with you between,
Surrounded by old trees and strolling cows,
  Staring through all your windows at the green.
Your homely floor is creaking for our tread;
  The smiling tea-pot with contented spout
Thinks of the boiling water, and the bread
  Longs for the butter. All their hands are out
    To greet us, and the gentle blankets seem
    Purring and crooning: " Lie in us, and dream."

II

The key will stammer, and the door reply,
  The hall wake, yawn, and smile; the torpid stair
Will grumble at our feet, the table cry:
  " Fetch my belongings for me; I am bare."
A clatter! Something in the attic falls.
  A ghost has lifted up his robes and fled.
The loitering shadows move along the walls;
  Then silence very slowly lifts his head.
The starling with impatient screech has flown
  The chimney, and is watching from the tree.
They thought us gone forever: mouse alone
  Stops in the middle of the floor to see.
    Now all you idle things, resume your toil.
    Hearth, put your flames on. Sulky kettle, boil.

III

Contented evening; comfortable joys;
  The snoozing fire, and all the fields are still:
Tranquil delight, no purpose, and no noise—
  Unless the slow wind flowing round the hill.
" Murry " (the kettle) dozes; little mouse
  Is rambling prudently round the floor.
There's lovely conversation in this house:
  Words become princes that were slaves before.
What a sweet atmosphere for you and me
  The people that have been here left behind . . .
Oh, but I fear it may turn out to be
  Built of a dream, erected in the mind:
    So if we speak too loud, we may awaken
    To find it vanished, and ourselves mistaken.

IV

Lift up the curtain carefully. All the trees
  Stand in the dark like drowsy sentinels.
The oak is talkative to-night; he tells
  The little bushes crowding at his knees
That formidable, hard, voluminous
  History of growth from acorn unto age.
They titter like school-children; they arouse
  Their comrades, who exclaim: " He is very sage."
Look how the moon is staring through that cloud,
  Laying and lifting idle streaks of light.
O hark! was that the monstrous wind, so loud
  And sudden, prowling always through the night?
    Let down the shaking curtain. They are queer,
    Those foreigners. They and we live so near.

V

Come, come to bed. The shadows move about,
  And someone seems to overhear our talk.
The fire is low; the candles flicker out;
  The ghosts of former tenants want to walk.
Already they are shuffling through the gloom.
  I felt an old man touch my shoulder-blade;
Once he was married here: they love this room,
  He and his woman and the child they made.
Dead, dead, they are, yet some familiar sound,
  Creeping along the brink of happy life,
Revives their memory from underground—
  The farmer and his troublesome old wife.
    Let us be going: as we climb the stairs,
    They'll sit down in our warm half-empty chairs.

VI

Morning! Wake up! Awaken! All the boughs
  Are rippling on the air across the green.
The youngest birds are singing in the house.
  Blood of the world!—and is the country clean?
Disturb the precinct. Cool it with a shout.
  Sing as you trundle down to light the fire.
Turn the encumbering shadows tumbling out,
  And fill the chambers with a new desire.
Life is no good, unless the morning brings
  White happiness and quick delight of day,
These half-inanimate domestic things
  Must all be useful, or must go away.
    Coffee, be fragrant. Porridge in my plate,
    Increase the vigour to fulfil my fate.

VII

The fresh air moves like water round a boat.
  The white clouds wander. Let us wander too.
The whining, wavering plover flap and float.
  That crow is flying after that cuckoo.
Look! Look! . . . They're gone. What are the great
    trees calling?
  Just come a little farther, by that edge
Of green, to where the stormy ploughland, falling
  Wave upon wave, is lapping to the hedge.
Oh, what a lovely bank! Give me your hand.
  Lie down and press your heart against the ground.
Let us both listen till we understand,
  Each through the other, every natural sound. . . .
    I can't hear anything to-day, can you,
    But, far and near, " Cuckoo! Cuckoo! Cuckoo!'

VIII

The everlasting grass—how bright, how cool!
  The day has gone too suddenly, too soon.
There's something white and shiny in that pool—
  Throw in a stone, and you will hit the moon.
Listen, the church-bell ringing! Do not say
  We must go back to-morrow to our work.
We'll tell them we are dead: we died to-day.
  We're lazy. We're too happy. We will shirk.
We're cows. We're kettles. We'll be anything
  Except the manikins of time and fear.
We'll start away to-morrow wandering,
  And nobody will notice in a year. . . .
    Now the great sun is slipping underground,
    Grip firmly! How the earth is whirling round.

IX

Be staid; be careful; and be not too free.
Temptation to enjoy your liberty
May rise against you, break into a crime,
And smash the habits of employing Time.
It serves no purpose that the careful clock
  Mark the appointment, the officious train
Hurry to keep it, if the minutes mock
  Loud in your ear: "Late. Late. Late. Late again."
Week-end is very well on Saturday:
  On Monday it's a different affair—
A little episode, a trivial stay
  In some oblivious spot somehow, somewhere.
    On Sunday night we hardly laugh or speak:
    Week-end begins to merge itself in Week.

X

Pack up the house, and close the creaking door.
  The fields are dull this morning in the rain.
It's difficult to leave that homely floor.
  Wave a light hand; we will return again.
(What was that bird?) Good-bye, ecstatic tree,
  Floating, bursting, and breathing on the air.
The lonely farm is wondering that we
  Can leave. How every window seems to stare!
That bag is heavy. Share it for a bit.
  You like that gentle swashing of the ground
As we tread? . . .
                It is over. Now we sit
  Reading the morning paper in the sound
    Of the debilitating heavy train.
    London again, again. London again.

Harold Monro.

In the study of a poem then, first listen to the poem without stopping to analyse the subject matter, reading it aloud, or silently at a speaking pace, shaping the sounds, either for the actual ear or for the ear of the mind. Then, find out what it is all about, searching for the literal meaning underlying the figures of speech; be able to give the subject briefly in a few words, and also, at greater length, trace the development and expansion of the poet's thought; and in doing so, be aware that the subject is rarely considered objectively, but that the poet's own feelings are involved. Try to get out of the poem all the meaning that he intended. With some poems this is easy; with others you may need more study, and perhaps some help with allusions. Here are three examples, two of which are very simple and straightforward:

COVERINGS

I

The snake had shed his brindled skin
To meet the marching feet of spring;
With bar, curve, loop and whirling ring
The patterned swathes, papyrus-thin,
Lay on the cage's sanded floor
Marked with the dragging python-spoor.

Flick-flack! Like ash or vulcanite
His lidless eyes in the spatulate
Head were alive with watchful hate,
Daring the sounds and the raw spring light.
He shone like watered silk from his tongue
To his tapering tail where the skin-shreds hung.

loudy yellow of mustard flowers
arred on his skin with jetty flares
ıe five-patched circle the leopard wears:
a-shell's convolute green towers
called to mind by his belly's hue
..at faded to pallid egg-shell blue.

He was covered so to face the sun;
That shadows of leaves might match his skin;
That, where the lily roots begin,
You might not see where the snake begun;
That Man might see, when Snake was dressed,
God in snake made manifest.

II

Mrs. Fand wore a fox round her wrinkled throat;
He was killed at dawn as he snarled his threat
In a bracken-brake where the mist lay wet.
Two men were drowned in a shattered boat
Hunting the whale for the silk-bound shred
That balanced her bust with her henna'd head.

An osprey's plume brushed her fallen chin,
And a lorgnette hung on a platinum chain
To deputise for her sightless brain.
Her high-heeled shoes were of python skin,
Her gloves of the gentle reindeer's hide,
And to make her card-case a lizard died.

She watched the flickering counter-play
As the snake reared up with tongue and eye
Licking the air for newt and fly;
And shook herself as she turned away
With a tolerant movement of her head:
" The nasty, horrid thing!" she said.

Stella Gibbons.

The poem is divided into two parts. The first part describes a snake in captivity. Having newly cast its skin, it appears now all shining and silken, patterned and coloured in such a way that it is perfectly camouflaged, not for its life in a cage, but for its natural surroundings of grass and leaves and sand, against which it must have been barely distinguishable. In its aloof beauty, it looks with contempt and hatred on the spectators who stare at it through the bars of its cage; it, like them, is one of God's creatures, but unlike them, it has been content with the coverings God gave it.

In the second part we meet one of the human beings. Mrs. Fand is dressed in clothes of men's devising, won at the expense of the lives of others of God's creatures. The skin of a murdered fox is round her neck; the whalebone of her corset cost two men's lives; a beautiful bird died to decorate her hat; a python, a reindeer and a lizard to provide her with shoes, gloves and hand-bag.

The poet echoes the snake's scorn for the woman, and is angry and bitterly contemptuous of her lack of claim to any beauty on her own account: her throat is wrinkled and her hair henna'd; her chin disappears in her neck and she cannot see without glasses. What a poor thing she is. And yet she dares to look at the snake—God's handiwork straight from the Maker's hands—and to shudder a little as she says: " The nasty, horrid thing!"

The imagery in this poem is wonderfully vivid in the picture of the snake, its old skin lying on the floor in folds, thin and dry, its new skin shining

" like watered silk " . . . but that is taking us into a realm which we shall explore later.

In the following picture of a drover, the poet has succeeded in concentrating not only the thoughts and feelings of an Irish peasant, but also the sum of the Irish character, countryside and climate: the imaginative and poetic fantasy of the Irishman, the strong understanding and knowledge of his cattle, the hot blood which breaks out in loud argument and violence; the barren countryside, either boggy or rocky; the dark peaty streams; and the soft west winds that make the grass lush and long.

The language is simple, but vivid and strong, and full of wonderfully descriptive adjectives. The metre, with its slow heavy beats, echoes the slow heavy trudging of the beasts. The poem seems itself to be warm with the breathing of the cattle, and moist with the soft wind off the sea; and beneath it all runs the mournful undertone characteristic of Irish song and poetry. But again we have overstepped the limits of " Subject ", so here is the poem:

A DROVER

To Meath of the pastures,
From wet hills by the sea,
Through Leitrim and Longford,
Go my cattle and me.

I hear in the darkness
Their slipping and breathing—

I name them the byways
They're to pass without heeding;

Then the wet, winding roads,
Brown bogs with black water,
And my thoughts on white ships
And the King o' Spain's daughter.

O farmer, strong farmer!
You can spend at the fair,
But your face you must turn
To your crops and your care;

And, soldiers, red soldiers!
You've seen many lands,
But you walk two by two,
And by captain's commands!

O the smell of the beasts,
The wet wind in the morn,
And the proud and hard earth
Never broken for corn!

And the crowds at the fair,
The herds loosened and blind,
Loud words and dark faces,
And the wild blood behind!

(O strong men with your best
I would strive breast to breast,
I could quiet your herds
With my words, with my words!)

I will bring you, my kine,
Where there's grass to the knee,

But you'll think of scant croppings
Harsh with salt of the sea.

Padraic Colum.

The following beautiful poem is less straightforward and obvious in its subject matter; the full implication and development of the poet's thought are not to be grasped by every reader at a first glance.

THE OLD SHIPS

I have seen old ships sail like swans asleep
Beyond the village which men still call Tyre,
With leaden age o'ercargoed, dipping deep
For Famagusta and the hidden sun
That rings black Cyprus with a lake of fire;
And all those ships were certainly so old
Who knows how oft with squat and noisy gun,
Questing brown slaves or Syrian oranges,
The pirate Genoese
Hell-raked them till they rolled
Blood, water, fruit and corpses up the hold.
But now through friendly seas they softly run,
Painted the mid-sea blue or shore-sea green,
Still patterned with the vine and grapes in gold.

But I have seen,
Pointing her shapely shadows from the dawn
And image tumbled on a rose-swept bay,
A drowsy ship of some yet older day;
And, wonder's breath indrawn,
Thought I—who knows—who knows—but in that same
(Fished up beyond Aeaea, patched up new
—Stern painted brighter blue—)

That talkative, bald-headed seaman came
(Twelve patient comrades sweating at the oar)
From Troy's doom-crimson shore,
And with great lies about his wooden horse
Set the crew laughing, and forgot his course.

It was so old a ship—who knows, who knows?
—And yet so beautiful, I watched in vain
To see the mast burst open with a rose,
And the whole deck put on its leaves again.

James Elroy Flecker.

The poet has seen " the old ships " of the title, going about their ordinary business, fetching and carrying and plying their trade in the eastern Mediterranean and the Ægean Sea, just as they did hundreds of years ago, when the Middle Sea was infested with pirates. It seems to the poet that these same ships, painted blue and green, bordered with the traditional ornament of grape and leaf in gold, now peacefully sailing from island to island, fought many a bloody battle to save their precious cargoes of fruit and slaves, from mediæval pirates. The poet's imagination is stirred by the romantic associations of these faded little craft, and of one in particular, older than the others, and much more beautiful, possibly the very ship in which Ulysses set out on his extended voyage home to Ithaca after the conclusion of the Trojan War. The poet sees the ship, faded now, but brightly painted then, rowed by twelve of Ulysses' comrades, while he, their leader, boasts of the success of the mighty wooden horse, a stratagem conceived by his own wily brain, which brought about the fall of Troy. In headlong stuttering speech which the poet suggests by broken lines, the hero relives his triumph. Left high and dry on the beach while the Grecian fleet set sail out of sight behind the island of Tenedos, the wooden horse held in its cavernous interior a band of armed men. The Trojans, deceived, dragged it into their city, which for ten years the Greeks had tried in vain to storm. In the dead of night, the hidden men descended and opened the gates to their comrades now returned. The doomed city was given over to fire and sword, and the siege was ended.

" It was so old a ship . . . and yet so beautiful ", that the poet almost expected to see the timbers quicken and burst forth into leaf and flower again:

> It was so old a ship—who knows—who knows?
> And yet so beautiful, I watched in vain
> To see the mast burst open with a rose,
> And the whole deck put on its leaves again.

Those are four of the loveliest lines ever written, and I have to confess that they sweep me off my feet. Are yours still firmly on the ground?

CHAPTER FOUR

"The Fire Kindles"

I held my tongue and spake nothing;
I kept silence, yea even from good words;
    but it was pain and grief to me.
My heart was hot within me, and while I was
    thus musing the fire kindled:
And at the last I spake with my tongue.

Psalm 39.

The first question we ask ourselves when studying a poem, is: What is it about? We are now about to ask the second—a multiple question: What made the poet write it? What was the source of his inspiration? What emotion did it rouse in him? What was his mood? What was his aim in writing it at all?

Of all the emotions that stir the human heart, love is the most constant and universal, and poets of all times have been inspired to write of it in all its aspects: happy love, hopeless love; love rewarded, love unrequited; young love, married love. The moods of the poet may be as varied: he may take his love seriously, gaily, sadly, flippantly, ironically; but whatever his mood, he must succeed in getting it across to you, the reader.

In any collection of modern lyrics you will find fewer love poems and a wider range of subjects than in the poetry of any other time; and much of what love poetry there is seems to have been inspired by disappointment. Are our poets less favoured by the fair than the poets of old, or is it that happy love lulls inspiration to sleep?

In the following poem by Yeats, the emotion is tinged more with regret than with deep sorrow; the tears are shed for a happiness lost along ago:

DOWN BY THE SALLEY GARDENS

Down by the salley gardens my love and I did meet;
She passed the salley gardens with little snow-white feet.
She bid me take love easy, as the leaves grow on the tree;
But I, being young and foolish, with her would not agree.

In a field by the river my love and I did stand,
And on my leaning shoulder she laid her snow-white hand.
She bid me take love easy, as the grass grows on the weirs;
But I was young and foolish, and now am full of tears.

W. B. Yeats.

The emotion in the next is more poignant: there is no remoteness about it, but an ever-present aching hopelessness:

O WOMAN OF MY LOVE

O woman of my love, I am walking with you on the
sand,
And the moon's white on the sand and the foam's white
on the sea;
And I am thinking my own thoughts, and your hand is
on my hand,
And your heart thinks by my side, and it's not thinking
of me.

O woman of my love, the world is narrow and wide,
And I wonder which is the lonelier of us two?
You are thinking of one who is near to your heart, and
far from your side;
I am thinking my own thoughts, and they are all thoughts
of you.

Arthur Symons.

The lover speaks from bitter experience of women's inconstancy, in this poem:

NEVER GIVE ALL THE HEART

Never give all the heart, for love
Will hardly seem worth thinking of
To passionate women if it seem
Certain, and they never dream
That it fades out from kiss to kiss;
For everything that's lovely is
But a brief, dreamy, kind delight.
O never give the heart outright,

For they, for all smooth lips can say,
Have given their hearts up to the play.
And who could play it well enough
If deaf and dumb and blind with love?
He that made this knows all the cost,
For he gave all his heart and lost.

William Butler Yeats.

Next comes the ballad of the lover who went on his way singing in spite of his heartache:

A BALLAD-MAKER

Once I loved a maiden fair,
Over the hills and far away,
Lands she had and lovers to spare,
Over the hills and far away.
And I was stooped and troubled sore,
And my face was pale, and the coat I wore
Was thin as my supper the night before,
Over the hills and far away.

Once I passed in the autumn late,
Over the hills and far away,
Her bawn and byre and painted gate,
Over the hills and far away.
She was leaning there in the twilight space,
Sweet sorrow was on her fair young face,
And her wistful eyes were away from the place—
Over the hills and far away.

Maybe she thought as she watched me come,
Over the hills and far away,

With my awkward stride, and my face so glum,
  Over the hills and far away.
" Spite of his stoop, he still is young;
They say that he goes the Shee among,
Ballads he makes, I've heard them sung,
  Over the hills and far away."

She gave me good night in gentle wise,
  Over the hills and far away,
Slyly lifting to mine, dark eyes,
  Over the hills and far away.
What could I do but stop and speak,
And she no longer proud but meek?
She plucked me a rose like her wild-rose cheek—
  Over the hills and far away.

To-morrow, Mavourneen, a steeveen weds,
  Over the hills and far away,
With corn in haggard and cattle in sheds,
  Over the hills and far away.
And I who have lost her—the dear, the rare—
Well, I got me this ballad to sing at the fair,
'Twill bring enough money to drown my care,
  Over the hills and far away.

Padraic Colum.

Let us end this group of love poems on a different note. Here is the expression of a deep and enduring love, growing richer with time:

THE FOLLY OF BEING COMFORTED

One that is ever kind said yesterday:
" Your well-beloved's hair has threads of grey,

And little shadows come about her eyes;
Time can but make it easier to be wise
Though now it seem impossible, and so
Patience is all that you have need of."

No,

I have not a crumb of comfort, not a grain.
Time can but make her beauty over again:
Because of that great nobleness of hers
The fire that stirs about her, when she stirs
Burns but more clearly. O she had not these ways
When all the wild summer was in her gaze.
O heart! O heart! if she'd but turn her head,
You'd know the folly of being comforted.

William Butler Yeats.

Have any of these poems spoken for you? If so, they will have torn your heart with renewed pain, but you will be able to repeat the lines again and again till the very eloquence of the words heals the hurt.

After Love, the theme which has most frequently inspired the poet, is Beauty in a hundred manifestations: perhaps most of all beauty in Nature, and especially Nature in springtime. Even now, when winter evenings, whether out-of-doors in the lights and glitter of city streets, or at home snug by a warm fireside, have a comfort and a charm not known a hundred and more years ago, the coming of spring brings a thrill to the heart, and makes the sap rise in more than the trees:

NOW THE FULL-THROATED DAFFODILS

Now the full-throated daffodils,
Our trumpeters in gold,
Call resurrection from the ground
And bid the year be told.

To-day the almond-tree turns pink,
The first flush of spring;
Winds loll and gossip through the town
Her secret whispering.

Now too the bird must try his voice
Upon the morning air;
Down drowsy avenues he cries
A novel great affair.

He tells of royalty to be;
How with her train of rose,
Summer to coronation comes
Through waving wild hedgerows.

To-day crowds quicken in a street,
The fish leaps in the flood:
Look there, gasometer rises,
And here bough swells to bud.

For our love's luck, our stowaway,
Stretches in his cabin;
Our youngster joy barely conceived
Shows up beneath the skin.

Our joy was but a gusty thing
Without sinew or wit,
An infant flyaway; but now
We make a man of it.

Cecil Day Lewis.

Did I say that the sap rises in more than the trees? Why, even stolid old gasometers swell with the upsurging of spring!

Other seasons, other flowers, all in turn inspire the poet; and it is not only the poet's emotion which is kindled into flame. Read the reply to the cautious thrifty advice of the poet, the reply of the Wild Broom exulting, glorying, spending itself madly, fiercely, to give thanks for its beauty:

WILD BROOM

O wasteful Broom,
Each spur and spire
A splendour outleaping, a flickering fire,
Thou wilt burn thyself out!
Why lavish thy gold
On this bleak hillside where no eyes behold,
Save the flitting birds, that pass unaware,
And the scuttering bunnies who never care?
Be thrifty, and keep for the bare, dark days
Some wisp of bright raiment, some spark of thy blaze!
Be wiser, O Broom!
Be wastrel no longer, but mindful of doom!

But the Broom—
I flame, I expire;
I am Beauty's plumage, my wings are a fire;
For a boon, neither buying nor sold,
I scatter my gold.
I have made this hillside one far-trumpeted shout.
Sky and field may behold,
And the wind-ragged rout
Of tumultuous clouds,

The passionate dawn, and the hurrying crowds
Of fear-stricken lives, they may pause, they may listen
To my pealing thanksgiving,
My clamouring glory, my fierce boughs that glisten
And blaze to dry scrub, as I perish by living.
Your chaffer I flout,
Your marts and your pricings, your wisdom I scout.
But oh, the mad joy as I burn myself out!

Edward Thompson.

Are you still reading the poems aloud, or " voicing " them to yourself? If not, how much you will have lost of this glorious poem.

Much modern poetry is inspired by sympathy for animals and birds, and indeed for all of God's creatures. Here are two poets moved by the urge to protect animals from harm, and filled with hate and rage against those that wilfully make them suffer:

STUPIDITY STREET

I saw with open eyes
  Singing birds sweet
Sold in the shops
  For the people to eat,
Sold in the shops of
  Stupidity Street.

I saw in vision
  The worm in the wheat,
And in the shops nothing
  For people to eat;
Nothing for sale in
  Stupidity Street.

Ralph Hodgson.

What poetic justice! If the people eat the birds that eat the worms, then the worms shall eat the corn and the people starve.

THE BELLS OF HEAVEN

'Twould ring the bells of Heaven
The wildest peal for years,
If Parson lost his senses
And people came to theirs,
And he and they together
Knelt down with angry prayers
For tamed and shabby tigers,
And dancing dogs and bears,
And wretched, blind pit ponies,
And little hunted hares.

Ralph Hodgson.

The poet's love of animals discriminates between those who prey and those who are preyed upon:

A CAT

She had a name among the children;
But no-one loved though someone owned
Her, locked her out of doors at bed-time,
And had her kittens duly drowned.

In Spring, nevertheless, this cat
Ate blackbirds, thrushes, nightingales,
And birds of bright voice and plume and flight,
As well as scraps from neighbours' pails.

I loathed and hated her for this;
One speckle on a thrush's breast
Was worth a million such; and yet
She lived long, till God gave her rest.

Edward Thomas.

And here is a caustic little poem by Humbert Wolfe. Notice the original simile with which it begins:

THE GREY SQUIRREL

Like a small grey
coffee-pot,
sits the squirrel.
He is not

all he should be,
kills by dozens
trees, and eats
his red-brown cousins.

The keeper on the
other hand,
who shot him, is
a Christian, and

loves his enemies,
which shows
the squirrel was not
one of those.

Humbert Wolfe.

During the war of 1914–18, many young soldiers who had gone from home filled with a glow of patriotic fervour and a belief that war is glorious, returned shocked, disillusioned, hating the waste and futility of it. Here is one poem on the horror of the trenches:

THE REAR-GUARD

Groping along the tunnel, step by step,
He winked his prying torch with patching glare
From side to side, and sniffed the unwholesome air.

Tins, boxes, bottles, shapes too vague to know,
A mirror smashed, the mattress from a bed;
And he, exploring fifty feet below
The rosy gloom of battle overhead.
Tripping, he grabbed the wall; saw someone lie
Humped at his feet, half-hidden by a rug,
And stopped to give the sleeper's arm a tug.
" I'm looking for headquarters." No reply.
" God blast your neck!" (For days he'd had no sleep.)
" Get up and guide me through this stinking place."
Savage, he kicked a soft, unanswering heap,
And flashed his beam across the livid face
Terribly glaring up, whose eyes yet wore
Agony dying hard ten days before;
And fists of fingers clutched a blackening wound.
Alone he staggered on until he found
Dawn's ghost that filtered down a shafted stair
To the dazed, muttering creatures underground
Who hear the boom of shells in muffled sound.
At last, with sweat of horror in his hair,
He climbed through darkness to the twilight air,
Unloading hell behind him step by step.

Siegfried Sassoon.

Wilfred Owen is another poet of disillusionment:

ANTHEM FOR DOOMED YOUTH

What passing-bells for these who die as cattle?
Only the monstrous anger of the guns.
Only the stuttering rifles' rapid rattle
Can patter out their hasty orisons.
No mockeries for them; no prayers nor bells,
Nor any voice of mourning save the choirs,—
The shrill, demented choirs of wailing shells;
And bugles calling for them from sad shires.

What candles may be held to speed them all?
Not in the hands of boys, but in their eyes
Shall shine the holy glimmer of good-byes.
The pallor of girls' brows shall be their pall;
Their flowers the tenderness of patient minds,
And each slow dusk a drawing-down of blinds.

Wilfred Owen.

GREATER LOVE

Red lips are not so red
  As the stained stones kissed by the English dead.
Kindness of wooed and wooer
Seems shame to their love pure.
O Love, your eyes lose lure
  When I behold eyes blinded in my stead!

Your slender attitude
  Trembles not exquisite like limbs knife-skewed,
Rolling and rolling there
Where God seems not to care;
Till the fierce love they bear
  Cramps them in death's extreme decrepitude.

Your voice sings not so soft,—
  Though even as wind murmuring through raftered loft,—
Your dear voice is not dear,
Gentle, and evening clear,
As theirs whom none now hear
  Now earth has stopped their piteous mouths that coughed.

Heart, you were never hot,
  Nor large, nor full like hearts made great with shot;
And though your hand be pale,
Paler are all which trail
Your cross through flame and hail:
  Weep, you may weep, for you may touch them not.

Wilfred Owen.

This young poet himself was one of those who died as cattle, in 1918.

Disillusion, pity, scorn, anger, contempt; joy, sorrow, ecstasy; love and hate; many are the emotions that kindle fire in the heart of the poet. His aim is to kindle the same fire in our hearts: to make us feel what he feels, to hate what he hates, to suffer as he suffers, and to find relief as he does:

Out of the white ash seven little blue flames;
Not so terrible is the heat.
Out of my burning heart seven pennillions;
And my heart is eased.

From *Robert Rideout's Pennillion*, in *Seven for a Secret* by Mary Webb.

CHAPTER FIVE

"The Lovely Vision"

TROY

I read last night with many pauses
—For the flesh is weak though the spirit be willing—
A book I bought for a pound and a shilling,
" The Trojan War's Economic Causes ",
Till slumber at last through my eyelids crept,
And I let the book fall from my hands and slept.
Then, as the hours of the night grew deep,
A dream came through the passes of sleep
Of the silly stories of Homer's telling:
The press of the ships, the gathering hum,
Iphigeneia dying dumb,
The Greek tents white on the Trojan shore,
Achilles' anger and Nestor's lore,
The dabbled hair of the heroes lying
Mid the peace of the dead and the groans of the dying,
Hector dragged through the battle's lust,
The locks of Priam down in the dust,
Andromache's agony, Ilion's fall,
And, over all,
The lovely vision of naked Helen.

Robin Flower.

In the realm of " feeling " the function of the poet is two-fold: he expresses his own personal emotion and tries to move us to share it; or with prophetic insight he catches our emotion and puts it into words for us. His power is even more magical in the realm of " seeing ", for his observation, enriched by his imagination, can make us see things we passed by before, and look in surprise at the most familiar objects with a newer, clearer vision:

> For all that is beneath the sun
> By magic he transfigures to
> A better sound, a finer view.

Not only can he transfigure the familiar, but he can recreate the past, and from the rich store of his imagination provide a background, and a setting in which the most prosaic object sparkles like a jewel. Is not this what Flecker did for a few battered trading ships? The power of his imagination set them racing over the Mediterranean waters doing bloody battle with murderous pirates, and then in a twinkling sent them further back, out of history into legend, to carry the Grecian war-weary veterans at long last back to their homes.

It is this same power that from the dry text of a book on—of all things!—the economic causes of the Trojan War, conjured up the living history of events, the tragic sequence of war and death; that clothed with flesh and blood the heroes of that ancient struggle—fierce Achilles, wise old Nestor, dishonoured Hector and piteous Priam; that set the whole alight with an intensity of emotion that blazed to its climax in:

> The lovely vision of naked Helen.

Economic causes indeed! The poet—and we—know better.

It is this same power that enables the poet to reproduce what cannot possibly be known—what is beyond man's experience: as Rupert Brooke did, when in his poem " The Fish " he described the sensations and emotions of a creature living in an element foreign to man. He starts by describing the sensuous delight of the cool water:

> In a cool and curving world he lies
> And ripples with dark ecstasies.

The fish's experience is bounded by the stream; his world is ever-flowing, ever-changing:

> Those silent waters weave for him
> A fluctuant mutable world and dim,
> Where wavering masses bulge and gape
> Mysterious, and shape to shape
> Dies momently through whorl and hollow.

The sun does not penetrate into the water which is translucent and dim; but in the gloomy depths colours are yet discernible, colours which seem blackness itself to our unaccustomed eyes, but the whole spectrum is there for the eye that can perceive the range of shades between darkness and deeper darkness. This is a fine descriptive and imaginative passage:

> The strange soft-handed depth subdues
> Drowned colour there, but black to hues,
> As death to living, decomposes—
> Red darkness of the heart of roses,

Blue brilliant from dead starless skies,
And gold that lies behind the eyes,
The unknown unnameable sightless white
That is the essential flame of night,
Lustreless purple, hooded green,
The myriad hues that lie between
Darkness and darkness. . . .

There the fish lives under the water, where there is no light, no warmth, no sound. But there is love:

The dark fire leaps along his blood;
Dateless and deathless, blind and still,
The intricate impulse works its will.

The fish knows ecstasy as well as we: he feels the delicious rhythm of the tides; he knows the music of the blood throbbing in his body, in his " dank sufficient heaven "; he knows the bliss of floating at peace in the water.

THE FISH

In a cool curving world he lies
And ripples with dark ecstasies.
The kind luxurious lapse and steal
Shapes all his universe to feel
And know and be; the clinging stream
Closes his memory, glooms his dream,
Who lips the roots o' the shore, and glides
Superb on unreturning tides.
Those silent waters weave for him
A fluctuant mutable world and dim.

Where wavering masses bulge and gape
Mysterious, and shape to shape
Dies momently through whorl and hollow,
And form and line and solid follow
Solid and line and form to dream
Fantastic down the eternal stream;
An obscure world, a shifting world,
Bulbous, or pulled to thin, or curled,
Or serpentine, or driving arrows,
Or serene slidings, or March narrows.
There slipping wave and shore are one,
And weed and mud. No ray of sun,
But glow to glow fades down the deep
(As dream to unknown dream in sleep);
Shaken translucency illumes
The hyaline of drifting glooms;
The strange soft-handed depth subdues
Drowned colour there, but black to hues
As death to living, decomposes—
Red darkness of the heart of roses,
Blue brilliant from dead starless skies,
And gold that lies behind the eyes,
The unknown unnameable sightless white
That is the essential flame of night,
Lustreless purple, hooded green,
The myriad hues that lie between
Darkness and darkness! . . .

And all's one,

Gentle, embracing, quiet, dun,
The world he rests in, world he knows,
Perpetual curving. Only—grows
An eddy in that ordered falling,
A knowledge from the gloom, a calling
Weed in the wave, gleam in the mud—
The dark fire leaps along his blood;

Dateless and deathless, blind and still,
The intricate impulse works its will;
His woven world drops back and he,
Sans providence, sans memory,
Unconscious and directly driven,
Fades to some dank sufficient heaven.

O world of lips, O world of laughter,
Where hope is fleet and thought flies after,
Of lights in the clear night, of cries
That drift along the wave and rise
Thin to the glittering stars above,
You know the hands, the eyes of love!
The strife of limbs, the sightless clinging,
The infinite distance, and the singing
Blown by the wind, a flame of sound,
The gleam, the flowers, and vast around
The horizon, and the heights above—
You know the sigh, the song of love!
But there the night is close, and there
Darkness is cold and strange and bare;
And the secret deeps are whisperless;
And rhythm is all deliciousness;
And joy is in the throbbing tide,
Whose intricate fingers beat and glide
In felt bewildering harmonies
Of trembling touch; and music is
The exquisite knocking of the blood.
Space is no more, under the mud;
His bliss is older than the sun.
Silent and straight, the waters run,
The lights, the cries, the willows dim,
And the dark tide are one with him.

Rupert Brooke.

What a priceless gift is this imagination, for it enriches and extends every experience almost beyond limit, and it enables the possessor to extract the subtlest and extremest enjoyment from all things seen or heard or read. By its aid the poet can help others to look through:

> . . . magic casements, opening on the foam
> Of perilous seas, in faery lands forlorn.

He does this by his use of " imagery "; that is, the creation of pictures in the mind's eye; and not only that, not only word-painting, but the calling up of unheard melodies to delight the ear of the imagination. As we shall see later, there are many kinds of imagery besides the pictorial and visual; there is imagery which appeals to the other senses —imagery of sound, scent, movement and touch.

The most obvious kind of visual imagery is straightforward word-painting. Do you remember for instance the fishmonger's slab in " Miss Thompson Goes Shopping "? Notice how the vividness depends upon the poet's accurate and detailed observation, and his skill in finding exactly the right words and phrases. Notice too, in this and other examples, the poet's effective use of colour:

> Great cods disposed upon the sill,
> Chilly and wet, with gaping gill,
> Flat head, glazed eye, and mute, uncouth,
> Shapeless, wan, old-woman's mouth.
> Next a row of soles and plaice
> With querulous and twisted face,

And red-eyed bloaters, golden-grey;
Smoked haddocks ranked in neat array;
A group of smelts that take the light
Like slips of rainbow, pearly bright;
Silver trout with rosy spots,
And coral shrimps with keen black dots
For eyes, and hard and jointed sheath
And crisp tails curving underneath.

Most imagery, however, is not mere word-painting: it is description charged with emotion, as in " The Quails ", you remember:

Downward they drift, one by one, like dark petals,
Slowly, listlessly falling
Into the mouth of horror:
The nets . . .
Where men come trampling and crying with bright lanterns,
Plucking their weak, entangled claws from the meshes of net,
Clutching the soft brown bodies mottled with olive,
Crushing the warm, fluttering flesh, in hands stained with blood,
Till their quivering hearts are stilled, and the bright eyes
That are like a polished agate, glaze in death.

Here the poet not only makes us see the trapping of the birds, but he makes us feel also the pity and horror of it.

There is feeling too—the animal's as well as the poet's—in Masefield's description of the hunt in " Reynard the Fox ". At the beginning, the quarry, full of strength and confidence in his speed, exults in the thrill of the chase; later, as the pace begins to tell, the fox's desperation, and the poet's (and the reader's) pity, grow more intense, until at the last, when feeling has become an agony of suspense, there is the frightful shock of the climax:

From REYNARD THE FOX

The fox was strong, he was full of running,
He could run for an hour and then be cunning,
But the cry behind him made him chill,
They were nearer now and they meant to kill.
They meant to run him until his blood
Clogged on his heart as his brush with mud,
Till his back bent up and his tongue hung flagging,
And his belly and brush were filthed from dragging.

. . . .

The pure clean air came sweet to his lungs,
Till he thought foul scorn of those crying tongues.
In a three mile more he would reach the haven
In the Wan Dyke croaked on by the raven.
In a three mile more he would make his berth
On the hard cool floor of a Wan Dyke earth,
Too deep for spade, too curved for terrier,
With the pride of the race to make rest the merrier.
In a three mile more he would reach his dream,
So his game heart gulped and he put on steam.

. . . .

Like a rocket shot to a ship ashore
The lean red bolt of his body tore,
Like a ripple of wind running swift on grass;
Like a shadow on wheat when a cloud blows past,
Like a turn at the buoy in a cutter sailing
When the bright green gleam lips white at the railing,

Like the April snake whipping back to sheath,
Like the gannets' hurtle on fish beneath,
Like a kestrel chasing, like a sickle reaping,
Like all things swooping, like all things sweeping,
Like a hound for stay, like a stag for swift.
With his shadow beside like spinning drift.

. . . .

In one mile more he would lie at rest,
So for one mile more he would go his best.
He reached the dip at the long droop's end
And he took what speed he had yet to spend.

. . . .

As he raced the corn towards Wan Dyke Brook
The pack had view of the way he took;
Robin hallooed from the downland's crest,
He capped them on till they did their best.
The quarter-mile to the Wan Brook's brink
Was raced as quick as a man can think.

. . . .

And here, as he ran to the huntsman's yelling,
The fox first felt that the pace was telling;
His body and lungs seemed all grown old,
His legs less certain, his heart less bold,
The hound-noise nearer, the hill-slope steeper,
The thud in the blood of his body deeper.
The pride in his speed, his joy in the race
Were withered away, for what use was pace?
He had run his best, and the hounds ran better,
Then the going worsened, the earth was wetter.
Then his brush drooped down till it sometimes dragged,
And his fur felt sick and his chest was tagged
With taggles of mud, and his pads seemed lead,
It was well for him he'd an earth ahead.

Down he went to the brook and over,
Out of the corn and into the clover,
Over the slope that the Wan Brook drains,
Past Battle Tump where they earthed the Danes,
Then up the hill that the Wan Dyke rings
Where the Sarsen Stones stand grand like kings.

. . . .

Seven Sarsens of granite grim,
As he ran them by they looked at him;
As he leaped the lip of their earthen paling
The hounds were gaining and he was failing.

. . . .

He passed the Sarsens, he left the spur,
He pressed uphill to the blasted fir,
He slipped as he leaped the hedge; he slithered.
" He's mine," thought Robin. " He's done, he's dithered."

. . . .

At the second attempt he cleared the fence,
He turned half-right where the gorse was dense,
He was leading the hounds by a furlong clear.
He was past his best, but his earth was near.
He ran up gorse to the spring of the ramp,
The steep green wall of the dead men's camp,
He sidled up it and scampered down
To the deep green ditch of the Dead Men's Town.

. . . .

Within, as he reached that soft green turf,
The wind, blowing lonely, moaned like surf,
Desolate ramparts rose up steep
On either side, for the ghosts to keep.
He raced the trench, past the rabbit warren,
Close-grown with moss which the wind made barren;

He passed the spring where the rushes spread,
And there in the stones was his earth ahead.
One last short burst upon failing feet—
There life lay waiting, so sweet, so sweet,
Rest in a darkness, balm for aches.

. . . .

The earth was stopped. It was barred with stakes.

. . . .

But that is not the end after all; the fox is not done yet. He turns aside and makes for another earth—a rabbit burrow not far away. But his luck is out. A couple of men with a ferret and a terrier pup are waiting to trap the rabbit. The fox swerves, the terrier after him, down into the spinney—a short chase, but enough, for the dog has killed the scent. It gives the fox a welcome respite, but he is viewed again and the hunt is up once more. Again the feeling rises to a fever of intensity, and again there is the shock of disappointment when yet another earth is stopped. But luckily, he is in country now which is thick with the scent of fox, and just as he lies waiting for the hounds to tear him in pieces, he realizes that they have picked up another scent; and we are as thankful as he is when at last he goes safely to ground:

The stars grew bright as the yews grew black,
The fox rose stiffly and stretched his back.
He flaired the air, then he padded out
To the valley below him, dark as doubt,
Winter-thin with the young green crops,
For old Cold Crendon and Hilcote Copse.

. . . .

The stars grew bright in the winter sky,
The wind came keen with a tang of frost,
The brook was troubled for new things lost,
The copse was happy for old things found,
The fox came home and he went to ground.

John Masefield.

Some day you must read the rest of this grand poem. It is full of amusing and racy descriptions: of the meet at the Cock and Pye, and the members of the Hunt: a clergyman from a neighbouring village, " round-bellied as a drinking-can "; his daughter Madge:

. . . on foot, flush-cheekt,
In broken hat and boots that leakt,
With bits of hay all over her,
Her plain face grinning at the stir.

The local parson is there with his wife and son; two bright young things on bicycles—" Jill and Joan the slayers "; and then " ' There he goes, his bloody Nibs ' "—old Farmer Bennett the woman-hater. Then the Squire and his three daughters; the Major, the doctor, the " Harold lads ", the Colways, Hugh and Polly—poor Polly who was killed by a fall from her grey mare just one month later; Ed Manor and his sons Nob, Cob and Bunny; the aristocracy represented by " the Godsdown tigress with her cub " (Lady Crowmarsh and Tommy); then John Hankerton, Tom Sparsholt, John Restrup, old Pete Gurney—and Uncle Tom Cobley and all!

Imagery then, as we have seen from these examples, is in the first place, the creating in words of imaginary pictures. The poet makes these more vivid by the use of " figures of speech—the rich embroidery of language ". The commonest figures used in visual imagery, are simile, metaphor and personification.

We use similes and metaphors every day of our lives, and worn-out coinage they are, most of them: " as cold as ice "; " as deaf as a post "; " as hard as nails "; " as good as gold "; we " let the cat out of the bag "; we " split hairs "; " bolt our meals " and " skim over the morning paper "; the lover " presses his suit " and " wears his heart on his sleeve " while the maiden " drops her eyes " or " scorches (or freezes) him with a look ". None of these expressions means in the least what it says, but they have long since lost their power to startle, or capture the attention. Once they came freshly coined from the mint and were rich and vivid, but constant use has blurred their bright image and destroyed their value. Fresh new metaphors and similes are a sign of virility in a language, and English has been peculiarly fortunate in the many different influences which have added to and enriched it, not least the influence of modern American colloquial speech which is full of metaphor, unbeautiful perhaps, but vivid and vigorous—a lusty young growth from the stately old parent stock. A good simile and a good metaphor, like a good poem, are born of acute and accurate observation married to imagination and power over words;

like poetry they are founded on both fact and fancy, and you may fairly judge a writer's poetic quality by the quality of his metaphors and similes.

Both simile and metaphor are based on comparison, by which we are made to see one thing in terms of another. To make his description more vivid, to make us see more easily and clearly, the poet calls up before our mind's eye the image of some familiar thing which possesses in a high degree the quality he wishes to emphasize. When Masefield, for instance, wishes to describe the speed and vigour of the fox, he calls up one image after another all embodying the idea of swiftness, and in a series of vivid similes, superimposes these upon the picture of the running fox:

> Like a rocket shot to a ship ashore
> The lean red bolt of his body tore,
> Like a ripple of wind running swift on grass;
> Like a shadow on wheat when a cloud blows past,
> Like a turn at the buoy in a cutter sailing
> When the bright green gleam lips white at the railing,
> Like the April snake whipping back to sheath,
> Like the gannets' hurtle on fish beneath,
> Like a kestrel chasing, like a sickle reaping,
> Like all things swooping, like all things sweeping,
> Like a hound for stay, like a stag for swift,
> With his shadow beside like spinning drift.

In a simile (and a metaphor) the image is always a double one, and to appreciate its effect one must allow the mind to be as a blank screen upon which the writer projects first one image and then another emphasizing and enriching the first.

In a simile the comparison is direct; in a metaphor it is implied. For example, in the next poem " Crucifixion of the Skyscraper " by J. Gould Fletcher, the poet might have said that laying out the foundations of a skyscraper is like the nailing of Christ to the cross, a simile that we should have thought very far-fetched and not at all eloquent; but he did something more startling. He does not mention Christ at all, but leaves it to the implication of the word " crucifixion " in his first metaphor, and for his second he uses the one word " nailing ". But by this simple means he creates the sense of outrage upon the body of solid rock as nails and rivets are hammered home by the hands of men. Then, like the crucifix, the skyscraper is raised on high, solemn and somehow sad, with a dignity and a grandeur beyond man's comprehension. And last, with the image in our mind of the lonely cross towering high over dark Olivet, we see it bathed in the glory of the radiance of Christ's godhood, as the skyscraper, with all its lighted windows, tier on tier, rises to the velvet sky " in flights of gold ". The two images are there all the time, first one and then the other, fading in and out, and it doesn't matter which is left last in your mind, for the poem is as much about the crucifixion as about the skyscraper. Here is the poem—judge for yourself:

CRUCIFIXION OF THE SKYSCRAPER

Men took the skyscraper
And nailed it to the rock. Each nerve and vein

Were searched by iron hammers. Hour on hour,
The bolts were riveted tighter. Steel and stone
Did what they could to quench the fiery core
That blazed within. Till when the work was done,
Solid as a sepulchre, square-rooted to the rock,
The skyscraper, a well-polished tomb of hope,
Guarded by busy throngs of acolytes,
Shouldered aside the sun. Within its walls
Men laid a little gold.

But yet not dead
However long battered by furious life,
However buried under tons of frozen weight
That structure was. At night when crowds no more
Jostled its angles, but the weary streets
Of a worn planet stared out at the stars;
Its towering strength grown ghostly, pure, remote,
Lone on the velvety night in flights of gold
The tower rose. The skyscraper dripped light.

J. Gould Fletcher.

Good similes and good metaphors have usually more than one point of comparison, and they should not be dismissed lightly but should be examined closely to find all the associations and characteristics implied. Then, they should be appropriate; they should reveal more beauty in the beautiful, and more oddity in the grotesque; for one incongruous simile, by calling up a grotesque image instead of a beautiful one, can destroy the whole poem.

The bride hath paced into the hall,
Red as a rose is she.

The image is one of beauty; but suppose, if you can, that Coleridge had written:

Red as a beet is she,

and what has happened to the lovely blushing bride?

The last two poems have more similes and metaphors than have been mentioned (I hope you have already picked out the others). Here are two poems which consist entirely of one prolonged or sustained metaphor. The first is " Say What You Will " by Edna St. Vincent Millay. This is an unconventional poem, in that the woman in it insists that she is older than she looks, and she glories in her maturity: she is a tree in autumn still lovely with foliage not yet fallen, and with one last rose clinging to the bough; but autumn it is, for there is frost in the air and the birds' winter migration has begun:

SAY WHAT YOU WILL

Say what you will, and scratch my heart to find
The roots of last year's roses in my breast;
I am as surely riper in my mind
As if the fruit stood in my stalls confessed.
Laugh at the unshed leaf, say what you will,
Call me in all things what I was before,
A flutterer in the wind, a woman still;
I tell you I am what I was and more.
My branches weigh me down, frost cleans the air,
My sky is black with small birds bearing south;
Say what you will, confuse me with fine care,

Put by my word as but an April truth—
Autumn is no less on me that a rose
Hugs the brown bough and sighs before it goes.

Edna St. Vincent Millay.

The second, by Charlotte Mew, is full of the despair of lost love: the lover's heart is likened to a city once beautiful, now ruined and deserted. Notice as you read, how the division into lines follows the development of the ideas, each line being one complete image which by association calls up the next. This evoking of images by association is obvious in the last three lines where the comparison with the city of Jerusalem calls up the memory of Christ weeping over it, so that only with the final image, do tears come at last.

I HAVE BEEN THROUGH THE GATES

His heart, to me, was a place of palaces and pinnacles and shining towers;
I saw it then as we see things in dreams,—I do not remember how long I slept;
I remember the trees, and the high, white walls, and how the sun was always on the towers;
The walls are standing to-day, and the gates: I have been through the gates, I have groped, I have crept
Back, back. There is dust in the streets, and blood; they are empty; darkness is over them;
His heart is a place with the lights gone out, forsaken by great winds and the heavenly rain, unclean and unswept,

Like the heart of the holy city, old, blind, beautiful
Jerusalem,
Over which Christ wept.

Charlotte Mew.

A third figure of speech closely related to metaphor, is personification, which gives to inanimate things the attributes of living people. See what a vivid picture Robert Bridges draws of trees in autumn, by personifying them:

> The lime hath stripped to the cold,
> And standeth naked above her yellow attire.

And see how much vigour and life and movement are added to the picture of the north wind, by representing it as a person raging and smiting:

> In a hurricane through the leaves he teareth,
> Raking the boughs and the leaves rending.

Incidentally, notice again the effective use of colour:

NORTH-WIND IN OCTOBER

In the golden glade the chestnuts are fallen all,
From the sered boughs of the oak the acorns fall:
The beech scatters her ruddy fire;
The lime hath stripped to the cold,
And standeth naked above her yellow attire:
The larch thinneth her spire
To lay the ways of the wood with cloth of gold.

Out of the golden-green and white
Of the brake the fir-trees stand upright

In the forest of flame, and wave aloft
To the blue of heaven their blue-green tuftings soft.
  But swiftly in shuddering gloom the splendours fail,
As the harrying North-wind beareth
A cloud of skirmishing hail
The grieved woodland to smite:
In a hurricane through the trees he teareth,
Raking the boughs and the leaves rending,
And whistleth to the descending
Blows of his icy flail.
Gold and snow he mixeth in spite,
And whirleth afar; as away on his winnowing flight
He passeth, and all again for awhile is bright.

Robert Bridges.

A vivid piece of personification by Sir John Squire tells a whole story in four lines:

PREMATURE SPRING

Out of her cave the venturous virgin crept,
  Thoughtlessly shedding flowers on every side:
Old Winter saw the grace of her and leapt;
  Touched by his ancient icy arms—she died.

Sir John Squire.

The next poem is full of unconventional imagery and startling examples of personification. It is an amazingly successful attempt to paint in words a composite of all Van Gogh's best-known pictures—you can see them one after another. The poem has the same colours, the same rippling, blown movement, the same anguished restlessness; you can see the poplars swinging backwards and forwards like huge paint-brushes, or like brooms sweeping the sky. Notice how the sky too is set moving by the transference to it of the epithet "swinging". Look at the striking image of the thick-set trees like Provençal peasants with hands on hips—the only stolidity in all that wild movement. Look at the colours of the trees on the mountain-side and the vivid simile in which the poet describes them.

WINDY DAY IN PROVENCE

The cypresses are looped with wind.
The poplars besom the swinging sky.
Squat dark trunks, hands on hips,
Plant their feet in the fleeting grass.

Across his face the sun's hair
In golden wantonness is blown.
The mauve down of mountain-spines
Ripples like cat's fur backward stroked.

Under the bridge the rods wag.
Over the bridge the wires sing.
The river round the stolid drums
Beats blue to green and green to gold.

Wind at wide hats like captured crows.
Wind at heart like running surf.
And wind upon the wild sky
Like Van Gogh's paintbrush wild with pain.

L. Aaronson.

Not all poetry (and this is especially true of modern poetry) aims at describing and creating beauty, and therefore not all imagery is beautiful. Fashions in imagery change, and poetry to-day is less sensuous and less intoxicating than that of Keats for example; the modern poet keeps a clear head and his feet are usually on the ground.

These are some examples of contemporary imagery:

From AN ECLOGUE FOR CHRISTMAS

The jaded calendar revolves,
Its nuts need oil, carbon chokes the valves,
The excess sugar of a diabetic culture
Rotting the nerve of life and literature;

and:

The tin toys of the hawker move on the pavement inch
by inch
Not knowing that they are wound up; it is better so
Than to be, like us, wound up and while running down
to know—;

and:

On all the traffic islands stand white globes like moons,
The city's haze is clouded amber that purrs and croons,
And tilting by the noble curve bus after tall bus comes
With an osculation of yellow light, with a glory like
chrysanthemums;

and:

The country gentry cannot change, they will die in their
shoes,

. . . .

They cannot live once their idols are turned out,
None of them can endure, for how could they possibly, without
The flotsam of private property, pekingese and polyanthus,
The good things which in the end turn to poison and pus,
Without the bandy chairs and the sugar in the silver tongs
And the inter-ripple and resonance of years of dinner-gongs?

Louis MacNeice.

The ultimate test of imagery is not whether it is beautiful, but whether it is suitable, and appropriate to the subject and mood of the poem. What do you think of these examples taken from some of T. S. Eliot's poems?

From THE LOVE SONG OF J. ALFRED PRUFROCK

The yellow fog that rubs its back upon the window-panes,
The yellow smoke that rubs its muzzle on the window-panes
Licked its tongue into the corners of the evening,
Lingered upon the pools that stand in drains,
Let fall upon its back the soot that falls from chimneys,
Slipped by the terrace, made a sudden leap,
And seeing that it was a soft October night,
Curled once about the house, and fell asleep.

And this one:

> . . . when I am formulated, sprawling on a pin,
> When I am pinned and wriggling on the wall,
> Then how should I begin
> To spit out all the butt-ends of my days and ways?

He uses the same cigarette-end metaphor in " Preludes I ":

> The winter evening settles down
> With smell of steaks in passageways.
> Six o'clock.
> The burnt-out ends of smoky days.
> And now a gusty shower wraps
> The grimy scraps
> Of withered leaves about your feet
> And newspapers from vacant lots;
> The showers beat
> On broken blinds and chimney-pots,
> And at the corner of the street
> A lonely cab-horse steams and stamps.
> And then the lighting of the lamps.

On second thoughts: is it a cigarette-end after all? Isn't it more suggestive of a burnt-out candle-end?

In this passage from " Rhapsody on a Windy Night ", the moon is not intended to have beauty: it is a sordid scene and experience that her feeble rays illumine; she herself is a withered old harlot:

> She winks a feeble eye,
> She smiles into corners.
> She smooths the hair of the grass.
> The moon has lost her memory.
> A washed-out small-pox cracks her face,

Her hand twists a paper rose,
That smells of dust and eau de Cologne,
She is alone
With all the old nocturnal smells
That cross and cross across her brain.

Here is another poem by Eliot, in which the metaphors create literally in a single word the gloom and damp despondency of a foggy working-day morning:

MORNING AT THE WINDOW

They are rattling breakfast plates in basement kitchens,
And along the trampled edges of the street
I am aware of the damp souls of housemaids
Sprouting despondently at area gates.

The brown waves of fog toss up to me
Twisted faces from the bottom of the street,
And tear from a passer-by with muddy skirts
An aimless smile that hovers in the air
And vanishes along the level of the roofs.

Perhaps you find this kind of poetry disconcerting. Yes, it is at first, like most innovations. But just as we start by disliking some new grotesque fashion in clothes, and then, because we see the shop-windows displaying it and other people wearing it, we come first to tolerate and then to be enthusiastic about it, until in fact our taste has changed or at any rate has widened to admit the new: in the same way with new poetry and new art of any kind, we become adjusted to it by meeting enough of it. Some of us are immediately attracted by what is new, without discrimination, but most of us need to wait until it becomes familiar, and then we feel more able to form judgments. My advice to you is not to wait until enough poetry in the modern manner has forced itself upon your notice, but to go out of your way to read more of it. You may fail to understand much of it, but even at this stage you should be able, even if you do not fully grasp the poem's theme and aim, at least to feel the mood of it, and to pick out and examine vivid examples of imagery. Take the " sprouting " housemaids, for instance. What do the lines call to mind?

> . . . damp souls of housemaids
> Sprouting despondently at area gates.

They make one think of potatoes sprouting in a dark cellar — putting out pallid, unhealthy-looking shoots, limp and waxen; and immediately one has a picture of depressed, over-worked slaveys in cellar kitchens. The housemaids Eliot is thinking of, may have been perfectly happy: there's lots of fun below-stairs and still more at the area-gate; but possibly the poet that morning felt depressed by the weather and by the thought of these, to him, unlovely lives. The imagery he uses eloquently expresses his own mood, and therefore it is appropriate and good. But on the other hand, when in " Prufrock " he says:

> . . . the evening is spread out against the sky
> Like a patient etherised upon a table,

one feels that the image is neither accurate nor effective. As an example of shock-tactics it is admirable, but shock for shock's sake is not a legitimate poetic device.

Be receptive then, and above all, give your imagination full play, but be critical too, and reject imagery which is incongruous and inappropriate.

To end the chapter, here are some poems, all containing good examples of imagery, of simile and metaphor and personification; of colour and movement and vivid description. Pick out the most striking passages and read them again and again. And occasionally go back to poems in earlier chapters, and re-read them in the light of what we have since discovered.

THE MATCH

He strikes a match—and instantly
The lovely flower of light,
The little flame of life in the vast night
Blossoming on the dead stick, fills his eyes
With something of a child's surprise;
And they, new-washed with wonder, gaze
In innocent amaze,
As on that early mystery
When out of Chaos and Old Night
God spake, and there was Light.

W. W. Gibson.

SNOWFALL

At dead of night they came again
On tip-toe, without any noise.
When morning cleared the window-pane
There stood a row of choir boys,

Tall and lifting to the sky
In shining vestments wrought of snow.
I listened half-expectantly
To hear a Bach adagio.

Your slender beauty, poplar choir,
Was not more lovely when you stood
Clothed in the merrier attire
Of Little John and Robin Hood!

Lilian Middleton.

BOMBING CASUALTIES

Dolls' faces are rosier but these were children
their eyes not glass but gleaming gristle
dark lenses in whose quick silvery glances
the sunlight quivered. These blenched lips
were warm once and bright with blood
but blood
held in a moist bleb of flesh
not spilt and spattered in tousled hair.

In these shadowy tresses
red petals did not always
thus clot and blacken to a scar.

These are dead faces.
Wasps' nests are not more wanly waxen
wood embers not so greyly ashen.

They are laid out in ranks
like paper lanterns that have fallen
after a night of riot
extinct in the dry morning air.

Herbert Read.

CHAPTER SIX

"Enchanted Sound"

THE RELEASE

All day he shoves the pasteboard in
The slick machine that turns out boxes,
A box a minute; and its din
Is all his music, as he stands
And feeds it; while his jaded brain
Moves only out and in again
With the slick motion of his hands,
Monotonously making boxes,
A box a minute—all his thoughts
A slick succession of empty boxes.

But, when night comes, and he is free
To play his fiddle, with the music
His whole soul moves to melody;
No more recalling day's dumb round,
His reckless spirit sweeps and whirls
On surging waves and dizzy swirls
And eddies of enchanted sound;
And in a flame-winged flight of music
Above the roofs and chimneys soars
To ride the starry tides of music.

W. W. Gibson.

I

> Heard melodies are sweet, but those unheard
> Are sweeter; therefore, ye soft pipes, play on;
> Not to the sensual ear, but, more endear'd,
> Pipe to the spirit ditties of no tone.

In his " Ode on a Grecian Urn " Keats apostrophizes one of the figures painted on the vase, a youth forever playing music never to be heard except in the imagination. Poetry has unheard music too: unheard that is, by the sensual ear, but ringing and echoing in the mind. It is easy enough to appreciate the actual music of words, if one takes the trouble (as one must) to shape them and to listen to them; but the overtones of suggested sound are not so easily discerned; and yet with them the poet builds up a background of music that can become more real than the actual sounds he uses to create it. The effect is similar to the superimposition of visual images by means of metaphor, simile and personification; but here, instead of a double image in the mind's eye, we have two musical themes which can be listened to separately at first, and then together, one acting as an accompaniment to the other.

The poet achieves this by the skilful use of the natural character of consonant and vowel sounds, and by a specialized use of them in alliteration, assonance and onomatopœia. Consonants and vowels, alone or combined with others, may be used to create almost any effect of sound: consonants may be harsh, soft, jarring or melodious;

vowels may be long and languorous or short and crisp; and the poet knows how to manipulate sounds so that in addition to the words which convey the sense, we hear the suggested sounds which illustrate or even imitate the sense. In his " Essay on Criticism " Pope both states the principle and illustrates it:

True ease in writing comes from art, not chance,
As those move easiest who have learn'd to dance.
'Tis not enough no harshness gives offence,
The sound must seem an echo to the sense:
Soft is the strain when Zephyr gently blows,
And the smooth stream in smoother numbers flows;
But when loud surges lash the sounding shore,
The hoarse, rough verse should like the torrent roar.

One of the figures used in sound imagery is alliteration, a device by which the poet emphasizes, by repetition, the effect of consonant sounds. In this poem " Silver " by Walter de la Mare, alliteration on the quiet " s " fills the poem with silence and peace:

SILVER

Slowly, silently, now the moon
Walks the night in her silver shoon;
This way, and that, she peers, and sees
Silver fruit upon silver trees;
One by one the casements catch
Her beams beneath the silvery thatch;
Couched in his kennel, like a log,
With paws of silver sleeps the dog;

From their shadowy cote the white breasts peep
Of doves in a silver-feathered sleep;
A harvest-mouse goes scampering by,
With silver claws, and silver eye;
And moveless fish in the water gleam,
By silver reeds in a silver stream.

Walter de la Mare.

The alliteration here, runs right through the whole poem; but usually it occurs on two or more words that are next to, or close to one another—a purely local alliteration, as in:

. . . filled with singing seas.

But alliteration does not come on initial letters only. Do not miss the more subtle examples of it where the sound is caught up again in the middle of a word; or perhaps it may alternate with alliteration on another consonant. In these two lines from "Ecstasy" by W. J. Turner, see how the alliteration on " c ", " l ", " m ", " r ", " n ", and both the " s " sounds (the hissing " s " and the buzzing " z ") are interwoven:

To catch the lulling mazy coralline roar
Of numberless caverns filled with singing seas.

Another figure of sound imagery, is onomatopœia, in which vowels and consonants are arranged so as to imitate the sound described. In " Morning Express " by Siegfried Sassoon, there is a passage which perfectly illustrates this:

Guard sounds a warning whistle, points to the clock
With brandished flag, and on his folded flock
Claps the last door: the monster grunts: " Enough!"
Tightening his load of links with pant and puff.

First there is the belch of white steam on " . . . grunts: ' Enough!' "; then in the next line we hear the jerk and clatter of the couplings one after the other taking the strain.

Here are two more poems about trains. Spender has had much the same inspiration as Sassoon, except that he goes with the train far out into the country, whereas Sassoon stays on the station platform. There is a similarity, too, in some of the imagery: " gliding like a queen " is reminiscent of " Morning Express ", and so is:

. . . she acquires mystery,
The luminous self-possession of ships on ocean.

In " The Express " as in " Morning Express " there is the contrast between the strong, heavy beat of the first impetus, followed by the smooth, rhythmical movement as the train gathers speed:

After the first powerful plain manifesto
The black statement of pistons, without more fuss
But gliding like a queen, she leaves the station.

Do you hear the hiss of steam on " manifesto "? As you read the poem, listen for all the familiar sounds of an express going at full speed.

THE EXPRESS

After the first powerful plain manifesto
The black statement of pistons, without more fuss
But gliding like a queen, she leaves the station.
Without bowing and with restrained unconcern
She passes the houses which humbly crowd outside,
The gasworks and at last the heavy page
Of death, printed by gravestones in the cemetery.
Beyond the town there lies the open country
Where, gathering speed, she acquires mystery,
The luminous self-possession of ships on ocean.
It is now she begins to sing—at first quite low,
Then loud, and at last with a jazzy madness—
The song of her whistle screaming at curves,
Of deafening tunnels, brakes, innumerable bolts.
And always light, aërial, underneath
Goes the elate metre of her wheels.
Steaming through metal landscape on her lines
She plunges new eras of wild happiness
Where speed throws up strange shapes, broad curves
And parallels clean like the steel of guns.
At last, further than Edinburgh or Rome,
Beyond the crest of the world, she reaches night
Where only a low streamline brightness
Of phosphorus on the tossing hills is white.
Ah, like a comet through flame she moves entranced
Wrapt in her music no bird song, no, nor bough
Breaking with honey buds, shall ever equal.

Stephen Spender.

The next poem is called " The Bridge ", but it is never static, for from the beginning, even before the train comes into sight, the poem is full of flying forward movement; the bridge "with one leap" spans the cutting; the railway lines sweep across it and vanish into the distance; even the day rushes across the sky—there is no pause in the universal movement. In addition to the speed, notice the sound, how it rises to a climax as it:

> . . . grows, and roars, and sweeps,
> Menacing! . . .

Then:

> Louder the throb and roar of wheels,
> The shout of speed, the shriek of steam;

until:

> . . . the ground
> Shudders and the bridge reels—

and the train is on us:

> . . . with a scream
> . . . .
> The train roars past—and, with a cry,
> Drowned in a flying howl of wind,
> Half-stifled in the smoke and blind,
> The plain,
> Shaken, exultant, unconfined,
> Rises, flows on, and follows, and sweeps by,
> Shrieking, to lose itself in distance and the sky.

There is no variation here—from beginning to end it rushes on and past us at express speed.

THE BRIDGE

Here, with one leap,
The bridge that spans the cutting; on its back
The load
Of the main road,
And under it the railway track.

Into the plains they sweep,
Into the solitary plains asleep,
The flowing lines, the parallels of steel—
Fringed with their narrow grass,
Into the plains they pass,
The flowing lines, like arms of mute appeal.

A cry
Prolonged across the earth—a call
To the remote horizons and the sky;
The whole east rushes down them with its light,
And the whole west receives them, with its pall
Of stars and night—
The flowing lines, the parallel lines of steel.

And with the fall
Of darkness, see! the red,
Bright anger of the signal, where it flares
Like a huge eye that stares
On some hid danger in the dark ahead.

A twang of wire—unseen
The signal drops; and, now instead
Of a red eye, a green.

Out of the silence grows
An iron thunder—grows, and roars, and sweeps,
Menacing! The plain
Suddenly leaps,
Startled, from its repose—
Alert and listening. Now, from the gloom
Of the soft distance, loom
Three lights, and over them, a brush
Of tawny flame and flying spark—
Three pointed lights that rush
Monstrous, upon the cringing dark.

And nearer, nearer, rolls the sound,
Louder the throb and roar of wheels,
The shout of speed, the shriek of steam;
The sloping bank,
Cut into flashing squares, gives back the clank
And grind of metal, while the ground
Shudders and the bridge reels—
As with a scream,
The train,
A rage of smoke, a laugh of fire,
A lighted anguish of desire,
A dream
Of gold and iron, of sound and flight,
Tumultuous roars across the night.

The train roars past—and, with a cry,
Drowned in a flying howl of wind,
Half-stifled in the smoke and blind,
The plain,
Shaken, exultant, unconfined,
Rises, flows on, and follows, and sweeps by,
Shrieking, to lose itself in distance and the sky.

John Redwood Anderson.

Belloc's poem "Tarantella" is an excellent example of the use of sounds. It is full of alliteration:

> Under the dark of the vine verandah.

There is imitation of the sound of both castanets and guitar:

> Snapping of the clapper to the spin
> Out and in—
> And the Ting, Tong, Tang of the guitar.

There is the quick gay dancing and laughter of the first part, emphasized by the use of short vowel sounds:

> Who hadn't got a penny
> And who weren't paying any,
> And the hammer at the doors and the Din.

Then in contrast, the heavy mournful echo of the long vowels in the last lines, with the "m" and the "nd" reverberating hollowly:

> Never more;
> Miranda
> Never more.
> Only the high peaks hoar:
> And Aragon a torrent at the door.
> No sound
> In the walls of the Halls where falls
> The tread
> Of the feet of the dead to the ground.
> No sound:
> Only the boom
> Of the far Waterfall like Doom.

Vowels may be arranged in varying sequences as the notes of a scale are arranged to make a melody; or one vowel sound may be made to echo again and again in what is known as "Assonance". When you say (and I hope you *will* say it and not merely read it) Turner's poem "Ecstasy", you may feel the pleasure there is in actually making the sounds, without knowing why; but on analysis, obviously it is the same pleasure that one derives from a snatch of melody—it is due to the variety and arrangement of the vowels used. To take the first stanza only: in line one there is such variety that no more than two of the vowel sounds are alike; in the second line, the only suspicion of similarity is between "sought" and "shore"; in lines three, four and five, there is an equally great variety, but now notice the recurrence of the "ee" sound, as though the musician struck again and again the note that pleased him. Be aware as you speak this poem of the physical pleasure there is in making sounds skilfully arranged and varied by the poet.

ECSTASY

I saw a frieze on whitest marble drawn
Of boys who sought for shells along the shore,
Their white feet shedding pallor in the sea,
The shallow sea, the spring-time sea of green
That faintly creamed against the cold, smooth pebbles.

The air was thin, their limbs were delicate,
The wind had graven their small eager hands

To feel the forests and the dark nights of Asia
Behind the purple bloom of the horizon,
Where sails would float and slowly melt away.

Their naked, pure, and grave, unbroken silence
Filled the soft air as gleaming, limpid water
Fills a spring sky those days when rain is lying
In shattered bright pools on the wind-dried roads,
And their sweet bodies were wind-purified.

One held a shell unto his shell-like ear
And there was music carven in his face,
His eyes half-closed, his lips just breaking open
To catch the lulling, mazy, coralline roar
Of numberless caverns filled with singing seas.

And all of them were hearkening as to singing
Of far-off voices thin and delicate,
Voices too fine for any mortal wind
To blow into the whorls of mortal ears—
And yet those sounds flowed from their grave,
sweet faces.

And as I looked I heard that delicate music,
And I became as grave, as calm, as still
As those carved boys. I stood upon that shore,
I felt the cool sea dream around my feet,
My eyes were staring at the far horizon;

And the wind came and purified my limbs,
And the stars came and set within my eyes,
And snowy clouds rested on my shoulders,
And the blue sky shimmered deep within me,
And I sang like a carven pipe of music.

W. J. Turner.

This poem is an excellent example of the creation of " heard melodies " and unheard music too. It describes a white marble frieze carved with great delicacy in low relief. Everything about the poem is delicate and restrained—the pale colour of the clean, pure marble, the suggestion of faint sounds heard by the carven figures, the exquisite beauty of the figures themselves, the stillness and calm of the cool sea, and the deep ecstasy which filled the poet.

The imagery makes us not only see the marble figures, but even hear the sounds that one boy is listening to in the shell he holds to his ear:

> One held a shell unto his shell-like ear
> And there was music carven in his face,
> His eyes half-closed, his lips just breaking open
> To catch the lulling, mazy, coralline roar
> Of numberless caverns filled with singing seas.

Let us analyse the sounds in those last two lines. " L " is a quiet lilting sound, which runs all through the poem (indeed the poem is one long alliteration on " l "); " m " and " n " have a soft deep murmur; " b " has the softness and hum of the " m ", and the same deep full tone, with a vibrant force of its own. The sound " s " is one of the most eloquent in our language. It has two sounds, both of them present in these lines: the hissing sound in " singing ", and the soft buzzing sound in " caverns ". Both are sounds it is possible to linger on, and when they are drawn out by long vowels, or given resonance by joining them to " m " and

" n ", the effect is to slow down the lines and to suggest languorous ease and silence, not broken, but made alive and throbbing with soft murmurous sound.

We know what the boy could hear in the shell—a low rumbling murmur, rising now and then to a louder reverberating boom. See how the poet suggests that variation by using first " c " to harden the sound, and then three rolling " r's " to deepen it, before he softens it again with the " n ", " m ", " b ", and " s " of:

> . . . numberless caverns filled with singing seas.

The other boys are listening to far-off, faint music. As the poet stood gazing at the marble frieze, the sound reached him too, and he experienced an uplifting of soul and sense that set the music thrilling through him in the purest ecstasy:

> And the wind came and purified my limbs,
> And the stars came and set within my eyes,
> And snowy clouds rested on my shoulders,
> And the blue sky shimmered deep within me,
> And I sang like a carven pipe of music.

Three Arts combine to make this poem: it is not merely written in words—it is carved in marble and set to music.

Here is another poem full of a very different kind of music. If you are beginning to develop your critical sense, you may decide that it is not so good a poem as " Ecstasy ", but it is an amazingly successful exercise in exploiting the aural and emotional effect of different consonants. It is full of contrasts: some lines are slow with long vowel sounds, and heavy with laboured consonants; others rattle along swiftly with a clatter of short vowels and three-syllabled words; some lines have a deadly monotony:

> Then a slow drub of bludgeon blows nigh clubbing;

while others are almost incredibly harsh and difficult to articulate:

> Until the sobbing strangles in the tangles
> Of crass embrangling creepers' throttling clutches,

which make one feel as though physically entangled in the toils of the tropical undergrowth. None of this is accidental. The poet has deliberately set out to give a sound picture of war-drums, and he succeeds in creating not only the sounds themselves, but also the effect they have on the hearer.

JUNGLE DRUMS

Huddling among the scared baboons, he watches
From his uneasy refuge in the boughs
The battle-royal as the lions roll,
A whirl of lashing tails and crashing limbs,
Round the contested carcase of the quarry,
But now, a lithe light-hearted springbok leaping
In the still crystal of the wizard moon;
When suddenly the snarls and skirls that rend
The tense expectancy of jungle-night,
Ripping his midriff, scooping out his vitals,
Stop dead—those steely clutching claws of sound
Blunted and muted to a thudded thrumming,

A far dull thudding, as of the jungle's heart-beat
Grown audible—the heart of occult evil
Pulsating with slow measured palpitation
Of sluggish blood, and the dumb sulking lions
Skulk through the bush, awed by that mesmerising
Monotonous redundant muttering menace,
Relinquishing their quarry that not even
One jackal stays to snuffle; and in the branches
No shuddering baboon beside him huddles,
All stolen off like silent ghosts unheeded,
As nearer, clearer, rolls that stunning drubbing,
A ghostly rub-a-dubbing like the drumming
Of ghostly marchers ever closer coming,
The bloodless drumming of a bony army
Beating again to unremembered battles
On the taut tympan of the tom-toms rattling
In cracking fusillades, then dully grumbling
Like sullen thunder in far hills, then rumbling
Like earthquake underfoot, then sharply shattering
The zenith with a cataract of clattering
That peters to a pattering stuttering mutter,
Now seeming but the pulse of his own terror
Feebly aflutter, now a spate full-flooding
The strained walls of his thudding breast to bursting,
Then a slow drub of bludgeon blows nigh clubbing
His senses to unconsciousness, then startling
His frayed and fretted nerves awake
With crackles as of burning brake,
Then sinking slowly to a lamentation
Throbbing and sobbing through the wizard moonlight
Until the sobbing strangles in the tangles
Of crass embrangling creepers' throttling clutches
And, suffocating under smothering lumber
Of centuries that crashed in crushing cumber
To a gross bloated fever-ridden slumber

Glutted with all the blood-lust of the jungle,
Is muted to a muffled moaning mumble
Droning and dulling to a silent stupor
More dread than death—then rousing of a sudden
A rattling roulade on his very eardrums,
Reverberating through his shuddering midriff
Rending each anguished fibre of his being
Till, just a stretched skin on earth's hollowed gourd,
He throbs and quivers, swinging at the thigh-bone
Of the old inexorable skull-faced Drummer
Madding the fearful hearts of men to war.

W. W. Gibson.

As with visual, so with sound imagery, the test is, not whether it is beautiful but whether it is appropriate. In a good poem all the elements must be in harmony and the imagery must be suited to the theme and the mood. Now, after a sound-picture of war-drums in the jungle, here is another of a different kind of music; there are drums in this poem too, but the purpose and atmosphere are completely different from the last, and therefore the sounds are appropriately softened and mellowed.

THE RIO GRANDE

By the Rio Grande
They dance no sarabande
On level banks like lawns above the glassy, lolling tide;
Nor sing they forlorn madrigals
Whose sad note stirs the sleeping gales
Till they wake among the trees, and shake the boughs,

And fright the nightingales;
But they dance in the city, down the public squares,
On the marble pavers with each colour laid in shares,
At the open church doors loud with light within,
At the bell's huge tolling,
By the river music, gurgling, thin,
Through the soft Brazilian air.
The Comendador and the Alguacil are there
On horseback, hid with feathers, loud and shrill
Blowing orders on their trumpets like a bird's sharp bill
Through boughs, like a bitter wind, calling
They shine like steady starlight while those other sparks
  are falling
In burnished armour, with their plumes of fire,
Tireless, while all others tire.
The noisy streets are empty and hushed is the town
To where, in the square, they dance and the band is
  playing;
Such a space of silence through the town to the river
That the water murmurs loud
Above the band and crowd together;
And the strains of the sarabande,
More lively than a madrigal,
Go hand in hand
Like the river and its waterfall
As the great Rio Grande rolls down to the sea.
Loud is the marimba's note
Above these half-salt waves,
And louder still the tympanum,
The plectrum and the kettle-drum,
Sullen and menacing
Do these brazen voices ring.
They ride outside,
Above the salt-sea's tide,
Till the ships at anchor there

Hear this enchantment
Of the soft Brazilian air,
By those Southern winds wafted,
Slow and gentle,
Their fierceness tempered
By the air that flows between.

Sacheverell Sitwell.

Robert Bridges is one of the most musical of poets. In these lovely verses to "Nightingales" there is no description of the birds' song, but the particularly beautiful and harmonious variation of vowel and melodious consonant sounds, makes the poem so satisfying to articulate, that it has itself all the beauty of the nightingale's song.

NIGHTINGALES

Beautiful must be the mountains whence ye come,
And bright in the fruitful valleys the streams wherefrom
Ye learn your song:
Where are those starry woods? O might I wander there,
Among the flowers, which in that heavenly air
Bloom the year long!

Nay, barren are those mountains and spent the streams:
Our song is the voice of desire, that haunts our dreams,
A throe of the heart,
Whose pining visions dim, forbidden hopes profound.
No dying cadence nor long sigh can sound,
For all our art.

Alone, aloud in the raptured ear of men
We pour our dark nocturnal secret; and then,
As night is withdrawn
From these sweet-springing meads and bursting boughs of May,
Dream, while the innumerable choir of day
Welcome the dawn.

Robert Bridges.

II

In addition to visual and sound imagery, there is also imagery that suggests movement or lack of it. We have had examples of both already in this chapter, but here are further illustrations in a poem by Edmund Blunden: first the movelessness of the pike is emphasized, and then, suddenly, the lines lengthen, and a succession of short vowel sounds creates a tremendous flurry of movement as the pike snatches at its prey.

THE PIKE

From shadows of rich oaks outpeer
The moss-green bastions of the weir,
Where the quick dipper forages
In elver-peopled crevices,
And a small runlet trickling down the sluice
Gossamer music tires not to unloose.

Else round the broad pool's hush
Nothing stirs,
Unless sometime a straggling heifer crush
Through the thronged spinney where the pheasant whirs;

Or martins in a flash
Come with wild mirth to dip their magical wings;
While in the shallow some doomed bulrush swings
At whose hid root the diver vole's teeth gnash.

And nigh this toppling reed, still as the dead
The great pike lies, the murderous patriarch
Watching the waterpit sheer-shelving dark,
Where through the plash his lithe bright vassals thread.

The rose-finned roach and bluish bream
And staring ruffe steal up the stream
Hard by their glutted tyrant, now
Still as a sunken bough.

He on the sandbank lies,
Sunning himself long hours
With stony gorgon eyes:
Westward the hot sun lowers.

Sudden the grey pike changes, and quivering poises for slaughter;
Intense terror wakens around him, the shoals scud away, but there chances
A chub unsuspecting; the prowling fins quicken, in fury he lances;
And the miller that opens the hatch stands amazed at the whirl in the water.

Edmund Blunden.

The next poem has a similar variation in speed. You should now be able to recognize this and to feel where the movement is slow, where it ceases, where it suddenly changes to lightning speed, where there is silence, and where sudden noise; and you should now be able to explain *how the poet does it*. And, although this is anticipating what we shall come to later, look out for the words that are most eloquent in creating the effect.

SNAKE

A snake came to my water-trough
On a hot, hot day, and I in pyjamas for the heat,
To drink there.

In the deep, strange-scented shade of the great dark carob-tree
I came down the steps with my pitcher
And must wait, must stand and wait, for there he was at the trough before me.

He reached down from a fissure in the earth-wall in the gloom
And trailed his yellow-brown slackness soft-bellied down, over the edge of the stone trough
And rested his throat upon the stone bottom,
And where the water had dripped from the tap, in a small clearness,
He sipped with his straight mouth,
Softly drank through his straight gums, into his slack long body,
Silently.

Someone was before me at my water-trough,
And I, like a second comer, waiting.

He lifted his head from his drinking, as cattle do,
And looked at me vaguely, as drinking cattle do,
And flickered his two-forked tongue from his lips, and
mused a moment,
And stooped and drank a little more,
Being earth-brown, earth-golden from the burning
bowels of the earth
On the day of Sicilian July, with Etna smoking.

The voice of my education said to me
He must be killed,
For in Sicily the black, black snakes are innocent, the
gold are venomous.

And voices in me said, if you were a man
You would take a stick and break him now, and finish
him off.

But must I confess how I liked him,
How glad I was he had come like a guest in quiet, to
drink at my water-trough
And depart peaceful, pacified, and thankless,
Into the burning bowels of this earth?

Was it cowardice, that I dared not kill him?
Was it perversity, that I longed to talk to him?
Was it humility, to feel so honoured?
I felt so honoured.

And yet those voices:
If you were not afraid, you would kill him!

And truly I was afraid, I was most afraid,
But even so, honoured still more
That he should seek my hospitality
From out the dark door of the secret earth.

He drank enough
And lifted his head, dreamily, as one who has drunken,
And flickered his tongue like a forked night on the air,
so black,
Seeming to lick his lips,
And looked around like a god, unseeing, into the air,
And slowly turned his head,
And slowly, very slowly, as if thrice adream,
Proceeded to draw his slow length curving round
And climb again the broken bank of my wall-face.

And as he put his head into that dreadful hole,
And as he slowly drew up, snake-easing his shoulders,
and entered farther,
A sort of horror, a sort of protest against his withdrawing into that horrid black hole,
Deliberately going into the blackness, and slowly
drawing himself after,
Overcame me now his back was turned.
I looked round, I put down my pitcher,
I picked up a clumsy log
And threw it at the water-trough with a clatter.

I think it did not hit him,
But suddenly that part of him that was left behind
convulsed in undignified haste,
Writhed like lightning, and was gone
Into the black hole, the earth-lipped fissure in the wall-front,
At which, in the intense still noon, I stared with fascination.

And immediately I regretted it.
I thought how paltry, how vulgar, what a mean act!
I despised myself and the voices of my accursed human
education.

And I thought of the albatross,
And I wished he would come back, my snake.

For he seemed to me again like a king,
Like a king in exile, uncrowned in the underworld,
Now due to be crowned again.

And so, I missed my chance with one of the lords
Of life.
And I have something to expiate;
A pettiness.

D. H. Lawrence.

Even now we are not finished with imagery, for there is lastly, though less frequently, the imagery that appeals to the senses of smell, touch and taste. There is something of it in " Miss Thompson Goes Shopping ":

Into the shop dim-lit and dense
With smells of polish and tanned hide.

Then the fishmonger's:

Whence is shed
So strong a smell of fishes dead
That people of a subtler sense
Hold their breath and hurry thence.

The smells in the chemist's shop are pleasanter:

The old strange fragrance filled the air,
A fragrance like the garden pink,
But tinged with vague medicinal stink
Of camphor, soap, new sponges, blent
With chloroform and violet scent.

And here is a poem with a wealth of imagery of colour, scent, sound and taste. Reduced to the prosaic, it is simply a catalogue of different kinds of honey and the appropriate season for each: in late March the bees find nectar in the willow-catkins and cherry blossoms; in April and May come the apple and hawthorn; in June the clover, sweeter than pink or honeysuckle; in mid-July the flower of the lime; and in August the heather.

HONEY HARVEST

Late in March, when the days are growing longer
  And sight of early green
Tells of the coming spring and suns grow stronger,
Round the pale willow-catkins there are seen
  The year's first honey-bees
Stealing the nectar; and bee-masters know
This for the first sign of the honey-flow.

Then in the dark hillsides the Cherry-trees
Gleam white with loads of blossom where the gleams
Of piled snow lately hung, and richer streams
The honey. Now, if chilly April days
Delay the Apple-blossom, and the May's
First week come in with sudden summer weather,
The Apple and the Hawthorn bloom together,
And all day long the plundering hordes go round
And every overweighted blossom nods.
But from that gathered essence they compound
Honey more sweet than nectar of the gods.

Those blossoms fall ere June, warm June that brings
The small white Clover. Field by scented field,

Round farms like islands in the rolling weald,
It spreads thick-flowering or in wildness springs
Short-stemmed upon the naked downs, to yield
A richer store of honey than the Rose,
The Pink, the Honeysuckle. Thence there flows
Nectar of clearest amber, redolent
  Of every flowery scent
That the warm wind upgathers as he goes.
In mid-July be ready for the noise
Of million bees in old Lime-avenues,
As though hot noon had found a droning voice
To ease her soul. Here for those busy crews
Green leaves and pale-stemmed clusters of green flowers
Build heavy-perfumed, cool, green-twilight bowers
Whence, load by load, through the long summer days
  They fill their glassy cells
With dark green honey, clear as chrysoprase,
Which housewives shun; but the bee-master tells
This brand is more delicious than all else.

In August-time, if moors are near at hand,
Be wise and in the evening-twilight load
Your hives upon a cart, and take the road
By night; that, ere the early dawn shall spring
And all the hills turn rosy with the Ling,
  Each waking hive may stand
Established in its new-appointed land
Without harm taken, and the earliest flights
Set out at once to loot the heathery heights.

That vintage of the Heather yields so dense
And glutinous a syrup that it foils
Him who would spare the comb and drain from thence
  Its dark, full-flavoured spoils:
For he must squeeze to wreck the beautiful

Frail edifice. Not otherwise he sacks
Those many-chambered palaces of wax.

Then let a choice of every kind be made,
And, labelled, set upon your storehouse racks—
Of Hawthorn-honey that of almond smacks:
The luscious Lime-tree-honey, green as jade:
Pale Willow-honey, hived by the first rover:
  That delicate honey culled
From Apple-blossom, that of sunlight tastes:
And sunlight-coloured honey of the Clover.
  Then, when the late year wastes,
When night falls early and the noon is dulled
  And the last warm days are over,
Unlock the store and to your table bring
Essence of every blossom of the spring.
And if, when wind has never ceased to blow
All night, you wake to roofs and trees becalmed
  In level wastes of snow,
Bring out the Lime-tree-honey, the embalmed
Soul of a lost July, or Heather-spiced
Brown-gleaming comb wherein sleeps crystallized
All the hot perfume of the heathery slope.
And, tasting and remembering, live in hope.

Martin Armstrong.

To conclude our study of Imagery, here is a poem, " Death of a Friar ", by Lascelles Abercrombie. It begins with a vivid simile comparing the ebbing life of the dying man to:

. . . any common coal that can
No longer heat the furnace . . .:
A cinder haunted by a twittering, dim,
Forsaking mutter of small, plucking flame.

To him appears the Queen of Heaven accompanied by three Angel Presences, who fill the poor cell with a blaze of light and colour, and with fragrance and sweet sound. The first Angel approaches with the first gift—a heavenly food which fills the dying man with an exquisite feeling of well-being. Perfectly relaxed, he experiences perfect rest, in a peace full of "living silences":

> No sound: but a continual passing by
> Of living silences; save, far or nigh,
> Some sound belonging to the silences
> Would drop like diamond; and chiefly these:
> Down falls of moss small water into wells
> Ringing in glassy little syllables;
> And quivering glides of cadence shrill and rare
> Of curlews whistling down the shining air.

Afraid of any higher bliss, unwillingly he wakes to receive the second gift: an intensification of sense that intoxicates him with delights, until all his senses are confused and intermingled as one:

> . . . Sense into sense
> Confused; . . .
> . . . the quire
> Of colours, and in flights of glistering fire
> The music there—amethyst, chrysolite,
> And topaz, reeds and strings and horns; and white,
> Whiter than moonlight on a sword, a noise
> Crystalline bright, like the singing of boys.

Then he rises above the senses, and becomes, himself, colour, light, music, and at last—out of the body—pure spirit. Then only, having experienced all joy short of Heaven, he returns to the body to receive the last gift—Death.

THE DEATH OF A FRIAR

So they would leave him there to die alone.
Why trouble more? All they could do was done;
Nothing but senseless breathing now remained
Of what the man had been. If death disdained
To notice his surrender, why should they,
Who never noticed yet the humble way
He had of living, dawdle to attend
Upon his humble dying to its end?
The unregarded serviceable man
Was finisht; any common coal that can
No longer heat the furnace was like him:
A cinder haunted by a twittering, dim,
Forsaking mutter of small, plucking flame.
And how long might it be, before there came
Negligent death contemptuously to bless
This lingering stir of mortal wretchedness
With one resolving touch, and on him cast
Mercy of cold and quietude at last?
The unregarded man had served his turn;
Some flickering round the cinder still might burn,
But 'twas a life dismisst: surely alone
He could be left to die.
When they were gone
Death came; but not in manner as they thought.
Suddenly he was awake and staring, wrought
Out of his lethargy to expect amazing
Presences there, by summons of a blazing
White and unspeakable astonishment,
That with a shatter like the lightning rent

The drowsy darkness of his dying mind.
His kindled spirit gazed abroad, to find
His cell a miracle: the magnificence
Of tawny fire crimson'd round him, whence
Gleam of delicious green played among blue,
Like heavenly flashes globed in sunlit dew;
And the air chimed, and changing fragrances
Were coolly fanned about him, as a breeze
Made by a pulse of great invisible wings
Drove spirits of flowers in sweet squanderings.
Then those he expected came: and first the Queen
Of Heaven, in all joyful light of green
Moving that ever glowed in grass or glanced
From falling water, and every blue entranced
In summer bliss of deep seas, and the height
Of air from April noon to June midnight.
So in her paradise she came, and shed
The colour of its climate round his bed.
But fire, and mighty fire, attended her,
Three tranquil majesties of fire; and where
Their golden pacing trod, there was no ground,
But gulf; for downward without end or bound
Vacancy open'd underneath their station,
And darkness of the world's annihilation
There burned more blinding than their white-hot wings.
Thus on the empty vanishing of things
The angels stood, Mary's obediences,
In fiery rank behind her loveliness;
Composed and patient their immortal zeal;
Their faces splendour as of molten steel;
Brightness in folds that thrill'd like scarlet heat
In silver, falling to their golden feet;
And in the steadfast flaming of their wings
A mounting ripple of fierce quiverings
Sparkling terribly—the infinite ascending

Of Fire unbeginning and unending,
Whereof their persons were the shapely flames.

In passion the man cried, as one who claims
Rescue with agony of all his strength,
"Mother of God, may I not die at length?"
Whether it music were he could not tell
That answered him, or an insensible
Piercing of ravishment into his brain;
But thus the meaning spoke: "Now for thy pain
Have thy reward! I bring electuaries,
Made of honey and such herbs that thrice,
Tasting of these, into delight extreme
Thou shalt be changed as ever heart could dream:
And they shall make it well with thee after all."
Askance, for fear the mere glimpse should appal
His seeing to a blank, beyond the bound
Of gleam delectable that sphered him round,
He eyed those glittering statures where they stood
Quietly ardent; and with a blench he could
See there were caskets in their dazzling hands.
But instantly they knew their Queen's commands;
And the first splendour of her ministry,
Bearing his casket of electuary,
Strode forth, making his way the yawn'd abyss
Beneath him; and as he near'd the bliss
The man lay in, the paradise of hues
That Mary loved him with, the sheltering blues
Mingled with sweet surprise of green, began
To glare a burning amber, and there ran
Through the translucency of azure shade
Reddening curls of lustre, and a blade
Of whitening vehemence: till the man sealed his sight
Against the full severe angelic light.

His service done, and Mary with his first
Of sacred food that poor heart having nurst,
Back to his place the stately angel went
To shine beside his brothers there; content,
As when his Queen her miracle began,
To wait upon her dealing with this man.

" Take now thy first delight!"
The signs of it
Were these: but the joy was an infinite
Exceeding its occasions, even these.
For stript from his life were labour and disease
Like unclean wrapping, and the shame to be
Indecent servitude to malady.
As if his flesh were all new exquisite sense
Assuming a divine experience,
Health was the thing he knew, health quick and beating.
Fine as a mind strange radiant beauty greeting,
His subtle body knew his health, and made
Bodily joy of it: joy his sinews said,
Muscles and skin and the hairs upon his skin,
Bones and the secret pith of the bones within,
Were intellectual speech of joy, and each
Marvelling distinctly in joyous speech
Of mere delighted faculty, aware
Of health, and the beauty of health. And long time there,
Receiving each elate particular glee
Of his brave body in serene harmony,
And passionately still, he lay intense,
Not to disturb the lucid affluence
Of health along the nerves of his delight:
Collected so in this, that even of sight
His will was jealous, and kept closed his eyes.
But slowly out to ampler boundaries

Rejoicing knowledge well'd its way; and soon
He knew where he was lying: and high noon
Above, and under him the crisp and spring
Of sheep-bit turf, and round him whispering
Short mountain grass to gentle mountain airs
He knew. Untouchable by men's affairs,
The great slope of the mountain held him high
And lonely, offered to sunlight and the sky.
There in his wholesome flesh he took his rest,
His eyes still shut: not seizure now of zest
That fastened every motion, but because
All his desires closed in this heavenly pause
Of rest perfected in the loftiest
Of light and air—his joy now all in rest,
And rest sensibly loving him from the profound
Of his hale body, and out of the vast surround
He felt unseeing of the mountain's day.
In mere simplicity of joy he lay.
No sight: no matter if the wind should teaze
Fleeces of cloud to thin white delicacies
Brusht clean across the blue in curve and stroke
(Loveliest thing to see), he would not look.
No sound: but a continual passing by
Of living silences; save, far or nigh,
Some sound belonging to the silences
Would drop like diamond; and chiefly these:
Down falls of moss small water into wells
Ringing in glassy little syllables;
And quivering glides of cadence shrill and rare
Of curlews whistling down the shining air.
There was the touch of power on his head,
The hand of the goddess; and it was into dread
She roused him, dread of any greater bliss:
" No more, no more! I want no more than this!
This was enough!"—the anguish of a child.

But Mary's love inexorably smiled;
The second angel came, and at his side
Gloried, and went back blazing to abide
In those devoted wings of throbbing fire,
A white-gold instinct one with her desire;
And with the second of the electuaries,
Fulfilling to the end her promises,
She bid the man: " Now take thy next delight!"
  Not to be named, but as to think starlight
Enlarging measurelessly circular
In utterance round the bright point of a star,
The tale of joys the man's life now must be.
Nay, such a speed and such perplexity
Of pleasured sense and mind's beatitude,
Not to be named at all, not understood,
No spectre of it fantastically kenn'd,
The joy his spirit came to in the end.
  It began sweetly. Fragrance to him stole,
With calling of blithe thrush and oriole,
From cherry orchards that a sauntering breeze
Has visited, when each garth of crowded trees
Is one broad mound of happy blossoming,
White as a cloud from the new heaven of spring
Fallen to lie on green. But sharper scent
Flowed in, dividing this mild air, and went
Spicing the inmost chambers of his brain:
Gorse steept in sunshine, sweetbrier in warm rain
Kindling of rosemary; and many more
Unknown: to odours that for tenderest core
Of feeling pry'd with searching nicety
Like spirit's smouldering fingers, now must he
Submit his being. Gust in his mouth, that past
Apples and honey, was power to hold fast
His saturated mind. Sense into sense
Confused; and medley of sweet excellence

Poured into him vibrating, like a tide
Taking a narrow harbour and magnified
In surging of its waters to be there:
Such thronging in, such narrowed turbulence were
The floods of delicate tumult in his mind,
The race in undistinguishable kind
Of the world's rapture into him: the quire
Of colours, and in flights of glistering fire
The music there—amethyst, chrysolite,
And topaz, reeds and strings and horns; and white,
Whiter than moonlight on a sword, a noise
Crystalline bright, like the singing of boys.
  Then out of sense he broke; no more by sense
He was aware, but his intelligence
Was now to Be, not know: life, conscious still
In thought and in a body incredible,
Became the beauty sense could only know:
Himself a sound of music—naked so
To all the pulses of rejoicing things,
Fibres of mind alike and bodily strings
Took trembling thence the passion of a sound;
And light he was, out of him glorying round
Issue of living light—the joy adoring
The gift of light become itself outpouring
Of answering light: his thought pure power of light,
And torrents of flashing particles icily bright
His blood, in limbs of flesh like fiery glass.
Not beyond this could vivid substance pass:
As if this speck of being, this body and mind,
In one essential energy combined
The shining din of the whole creature of light
And music of the burning world's delight.
  Then something new and nameless: a caress
Blandishing dark and silent all the stress
Of joys intelligible, and through him sending

Blissful dissolution and an ending.
And he was free, thoughtless and bodiless,
Having no form, acknowledging no place:
A speed, a phantom speed for ever fleeing,
Speed the uttermost purity of being,
Speed the imperishable thing in things,
The changeless ghost about which changeably clings
The growth and dying of the world: in speed
Out of the momentary man is freed
Unquenchable phantom purity of being,
The speed beyond the world for ever fleeing.

Once more where Mary and her angels stood,
The panting body and the pelting blood
And the confounded mind came back to be
Of common men the common misery;
But he by mighty memory pursued—
Longing to have it, and fearful lest it should
Descend on him. But more he durst not know:
" O let me be! Thou wilt not give me, no,
Thou must not give me more! For I have been
Where no more can be borne: O dost thou mean
To kill me with delight?"—The Queen of Heaven
Impassibly smiled: " More shall yet be given.
There is a third delight."—And by him stands
Now the third angel: in the blinding hands
The third electuary.
And heaven was gone;
And in his last delight he lay alone.
The morning found his blessed face, and there
The joy that is too great for life to bear.

Lascelles Abercrombie.

CHAPTER SEVEN

" Words, Words, Words "

THUNDERSTORMS

My mind has thunderstorms,
  That brood for heavy hours:
Until they rain me words,
  My thoughts are drooping flowers
And sulking silent birds.

Yet come, dark thunderstorms,
  And brood your heavy hours;
For when you rain me words,
  My thoughts are dancing flowers
And joyful singing birds.

W. H. Davies.

WORDS

Out of us all
That make rhymes,
Will you choose
Sometimes—
As the winds use
A crack in the wall
Or a drain,
Their joy or their pain
To whistle through—
Choose me,
You English words?

I know you:
You are light as dreams,
Tough as oak,
Precious as gold,
As poppies and corn,
Or an old cloak;
Sweet as our birds
To the ear,
As the burnet rose

In the heat
Of Midsummer:
Strange as the races
Of dead and unborn:
Strange and sweet
Equally,
And familiar,
To the eye,
As the dearest faces
That a man knows,
And as lost homes are:
But though older far
Than oldest yew,—
As our hills are, old,—
Worn new
Again and again:
Young as our streams
After rain:
And as dear
As the earth which you prove
That we love.

Make me content
With some sweetness
From Wales,

Whose nightingales
Have no wings,—
From Wiltshire and Kent
And Herefordshire,
And the villages there,—
From the names, and the things
No less.
Let me sometimes dance
With you,
Or climb,
Or stand perchance
In ecstasy,
Fixed and free
In a rhyme,
As poets do.

Edward Thomas.

I

We have not yet travelled far enough to say what is the difference between prose and poetry. The difference is not one of subject, for contemporary verse shows that the poet feels himself completely free to write about any subject that inspires him. Nor is the difference one of mood and imagination, for prose can express feeling in terms of imagery as vivid as the poet's. The trouble is, that while between prose and *verse* there is a clearly defined boundary (the difference is one of form only), between prose and *poetry* there is no such thing, but an indeterminate no-man's land in which we find so-called " poetical prose ", and, if you like, a good deal of " prosaic poetry ".

Nor is the problem brought any nearer solution by a consideration of language, for there is no such thing as a poetic language distinct from ordinary speech. Time after time in the history of the development of English poetry, language has tended to crystallize into a " poetic diction " sometimes absurdly far removed from the everyday speech of the people; and inevitably, time after time, poets have rebelled against it, and have striven to free themselves from its limitations. In the eighteenth century the accepted idea was, not that a rose by any other name would smell as sweet, but that it would smell a good deal sweeter; so birds became " feathered songsters ", and fishes the " finny tribe ", and the most simple objects appeared under similar elegant disguises. Wordsworth and Coleridge headed the movement back to simplicity of diction, and stripped poetry of artificial and conventional trimmings. But before another hundred years had passed, the crystallizing process had set in again, and the " bowers " and " groves " that in Wordsworth's day were so fresh and simple, had by now become as much a poetic jargon as the other.

Poets of our own day are again in revolt, and are again engaged in the task of bringing the language of poetry closer to the ordinary spoken word. You will perhaps decide that some of them go too far (as did Wordsworth on occasion). It is a common tendency, in avoiding one extreme, to swing too far in the opposite direction, and often the poet, distrusting verbiage as he does sentimentality, errs on the side of coldness, and understates his own emotion—although, as the next poem shows, the very baldness of the statement gives a greater dramatic shock to it.

BREAKFAST

We ate our breakfast lying on our backs
Because the shells were screeching overhead.
I bet a rasher to a loaf of bread
That Hull United would beat Halifax
When Jimmy Stainthorpe played full-back instead
Of Billy Bradford. Ginger raised his head
And cursed, and took the bet, and dropt back dead.
We ate our breakfast lying on our backs
Because the shells were screeching overhead.

W. W. Gibson.

There is no such thing as a special language for poetry. The poet expresses himself in what he considers are the best possible words and arrangements of words. They may be extremely simple; they may be so simple as to be homely; they may even be in dialect. On the other hand, they may be lofty and learned; they may be so learned as to need careful study before the meaning can be fully understood. But whatever the words and style of the writer, the test must be: " Are they suitable and appropriate to the subject and the mood?"—the same test, you remember, that must be applied to imagery.

The purpose of language is to convey meaning in the best possible way, and that alone should be your criterion. If the poet's meaning is obscure, it does not follow that the poem is bad: it only means that a greater effort must be made to find the meaning. There are degrees of difficulty in poetry as in all writing, because there are different degrees of mental quality. We cannot always understand the expression of a mind subtler and more learned than our own, or of an experience and an environment that is different from ours. We may not have the skill or the imagination to follow the poet all the way into the inner world of the spirit into which he may have penetrated, and we must admit that the lack may be in us and not in the poem. So do not make your ability to interpret the theme the ultimate test of a good poem, but *do* be critical of conventional, poetical jargon, of stereotyped expressions, of clichés, of colourless and redundant phrases, of words used only because they rhyme or fit the metre, and not because they are the best words possible. All these are the marks by which you may recognize inferior verse. Can you detect right now, the difference in the quality of the language—in the skill in handling words, between this:

> And yet thoughts however incomplete they be
> rise in my heart and comfort me,
> finding expression in the pale green leaves,
> the slow sway of the golden sheaves,
> caught in the flight of a twisting bird,
> shaped in sound by the hopeful word
> that has no need to steal its breath.

From *Hymn of Youth* by *Ronald Howie.*

and this by Wordsworth:

What crowd is this? What have we here! We must not
pass it by;
A Telescope upon its frame, and pointed to the sky:
Long is it as a barber's pole, or mast of little boat,
Some little pleasure-skiff, that doth on Thames's water
float.

The Showman chooses well his place, 'tis Leicester's
busy Square;
And is as happy in his night, for the heavens are blue
and fair;
Calm, though impatient, is the crowd; each stands
ready with the fee,
And envies him that's looking;—what an insight must
it be!

Never judge a poem only by the name attached to it, for few writers but slip occasionally; and I hope you have recognized the real felicity of expression there is in the first extract, and the commonplace pedestrian language of the second.

How exactly is this felicity in the use of words achieved? It is not due to the use of a special language which is of its nature pleasing, but to a happy selection and arrangement of words in common use. Here is a poem by W. H. Davies, preeminently the poet of simplicity; in words almost all of one syllable, he sets forth his simple philosophy.

LEISURE

What is this life if, full of care,
We have no time to stand and stare?

No time to stand beneath the boughs
And stare as long as sheep or cows.

No time to see, in broad daylight,
Streams full of stars, like skies at night.

No time to turn at Beauty's glance,
And watch her feet, how they can dance.

No time to wait till her mouth can
Enrich that smile her eyes began.

A poor life this if, full of care,
We have no time to stand and stare.

W. H. Davies.

Here on the other hand, is a poem about a fat woman laughing—a simple enough subject, but treated by the poet as if it were a world-shattering event, and therefore the language, appropriately, is far from simple.

MRS. REECE LAUGHS

Laughter, with us, is no great undertaking,
A sudden wave that breaks and dies in breaking.
Laughter, with Mrs. Reece, is much less simple:
It germinates, it spreads, dimple by dimple,
From small beginnings, things of easy girth,
To formidable redundancies of mirth.
Clusters of subterranean chuckles rise
And presently the circles of her eyes
Close into slits, and all the woman heaves

As a great elm with all its mounds of leaves
Wallows before the storm. From hidden sources
A mustering of blind volcanic forces
Takes her and shakes her till she sobs and gapes.
Then all that load of bottled mirth escapes
In one wild crow, a lifting of huge hands,
And creaking stays, and visage that expands
In scarlet ridge and furrow. Thence collapse,
A hanging head. a feeble hand that flaps
An apron-end to stir an air and waft
A steaming face. And Mrs. Reece has laughed.

Martin Armstrong.

These two poems, incidentally, illustrate the two chief strains in our language—Teutonic and Romance: the first, homely, domestic, and Anglo-Saxon, resulting from the invasion of Britain between the fifth and tenth centuries by successive bands of Jutes, Angles, Saxons and Danes; the second, cultured, elegant and Latin, deriving either directly as a result of the establishment of Christianity through the agency of Roman missionaries, and later as a result of the Renaissance, or indirectly through the Norman-French of those invaders who proved to be the last conquerors of this island, in 1066. For a considerable period after the Norman Conquest, two languages, French and English, continued to be spoken, one by the native population, and the other by their lords and masters. In this circumstance lies the explanation of the fact that our language is so rich in synonyms, since for every word of Anglo-Saxon origin, we may expect to find an equivalent derived from Latin. Speaking broadly, the former are short (often monosyllables) while the latter are usually longer. The Saxon words, while lacking the grace and sonorous beauty of the Latin, are direct, virile, and sturdy. They are the words of handicraft and farming (not of "manual labour" and "agriculture"); of the tiller of the soil, and of the chisel and the plough; of the housewife making butter and cheese and bread for her man and her children. Judge of their quality by this poem, and try if you like, the effect of substituting Latin words for the Saxon.

A SAXON SONG

Tools with the comely names,
Mattock and scythe and spade,
Couth and bitter as flames,
Clean, and bowed in the blade,—
A man and his tools make a man and his trade.

Breadth of the English shires,
Hummock and kame and mead,
Tank of the reeking byres,
Land of the English breed,—
A man and his land make a man and his creed.

Leisurely flocks and herds,
Cool-eyed cattle that come
Mildly to wonted words,
Swine that in orchards roam,—
A man and his beasts make a man and his home.

Children sturdy and flaxen
Shouting in brotherly strife,
Like the land they are Saxon,
Sons of a man and his wife,—
For a man and his loves make a man and his life.

V. Sackville-West.

However deep and poignant the poet's emotion, however sacred his subject, he can find simple words to speak for him:

REQUIESCAT

Tread lightly, she is near
Under the snow,
Speak gently, she can hear
The daisies grow.

All her bright golden hair
Tarnished with rust,
She that was young and fair
Fallen to dust.

Lily-like, white as snow,
She hardly knew
She was a woman, so
Sweetly she grew.

Coffin-board, heavy stone,
Lie on her breast,
I vex my heart alone,
She is at rest.

Peace, Peace, she cannot hear
  Lyre or sonnet,
All my life's buried here,
  Heap earth upon it.

Oscar Wilde.

Many poets go a good deal further in their desire to bring poetry closer to the people, and (sometimes in amusing contrast) make use of the most homely and colloquial language. In the next poem, contrasting with passages of beautiful imagery, are amusing interpolations in the vernacular:

MRS. HAGUE

Old Mrs. Hague,
The Gardener's wife,
Was not to be enclosed in any formulas.
She seems to stand upon a little mound
Of pansies,
    Primroses,
        And primulas.
Outlined against the pale blue eye of northern spring,
Heavily planted in this printed muslin beauty
Of clumps and spots and dots and tigerstripes,
She swelled with ideas and ideals of duty,
Emphatic,
    Rheumatic.

Mrs. Thatch,
The wife, she was sorry to say,
Of Lord X's gardener
—If such one could call him—

Was silly, town-bred, what Mrs. Hague would call
—Well, she really did not like to say it,
Did not know what to call it;
Shall we say a Ne'er-do-Well?
And all the time the primroses, the wind-flowers
Opened their eyes and pressed their nodding heads
Against her, and the moss seemed ready to
Run up those rugged limbs,
The lichen ready
To crystallize its feathery formations
Along these solid branches.

If not upon this flower-sprinkled mound,
Then Mrs. Hague stood
Pressed in the narrow framework of her door,
And fills it to our minds for evermore.
Out of the slender gaps
Between the figure and its frame,
Was wafted the crusty, country odour
Of new bread,
Which was but one blossom of the hedges
That Mrs. Hague had planted.
For Mrs. Hague was childless,
And so had wisely broken up her life
With fences of her own construction,
Above which she would peer
With bovine grace,
Kind nose, kind eyes
Wide open in wide face.
For
  Monday was Washing Day,
  Tuesday was Baking Day,
  Wednesday h'Alfred 'as 'is dinner h'early,
  Thursday was Baking Day again,
  Friday was a busy day, a very busy day,

And Saturday prepared the way for Sunday,
Black satin bosoms and a brooch,
A bonnet and a Bible.

Nor were these all:
There were other more imposing barriers
Of Strawberry Jam in June
And Blackberry Jelly in October:
For each fruit contributed a hedge
To the garden of Mrs. Hague's days.

These fences made life safe for Mrs. Hague;
Each barrier of washing, mending, baking
Was a barricade
Thrown up against being lonely or afraid.
This infinite perspective
—The week, the month, the year—
Showed in the narrow gaps
Between her and the door,
As she stood there in the doorway,
Narrow as a coffin.

Oh, who can describe the grace of Mrs. Hague,
A Mrs. Noah limned by Botticelli,
'Mid flowering trees, green winds and pensive flowers;
A Rousseau portrait, inflated by Picasso;
Or seen in summer,
As through a tapestry
Of pool, exotic flower and conifer?

As Daphne was transformed into a tree,
So some old elm had turned to Mrs. Hague,
Thick bole, wide arms and rustic dignity.

Osbert Sitwell.

Some poets go further still and express themselves in the dialect of their own particular countryside, and so long as it can be understood without too many footnotes, it is as powerfully expressive as any other form of words. There are any number of poems written in Scottish and Irish dialect, and in many English dialects; but here is one in French-Canadian:

THE WRECK OF THE *JULIE PLANTE*

(A LEGEND OF LAC ST. PIERRE)

On wan dark night on Lac St. Pierre,
  De win' she blow, blow, blow,
An' de crew of de wood-scow *Julie Plante*
  Got scar't an' run below—
For de win' she blow lik' hurricane,
  Bimeby she blow some more,
An' de scow bus' up on Lac St. Pierre
  Wan arpent from de shore.

De captinne walk on de front deck,
  An' walk de hin' deck too—
He call de crew from up de hole,
  He call de cook also.
De cook she's name was Rosie,
  She come from Montreal,
Was chambermaid on lumber-barge
  On de Grande Lachine Canal.

De win' she blow from nor'-eas'-wes',
  De sout' win' she blow too,
W'en Rosie cry, "Mon cher captinne,
  Mon cher, w'at I shall do?"

De captinne t'row de beeg ankerre,
But still de scow she dreef:
De crew he can't pass on de shore
Becos' he los' hees skeef.

De night was dark lak' wan black cat,
De wave run high an' fas',
W'en de captinne tak' de Rosie girl
An' tie her to de mas'.
Den he also tak' de life-preserve,
An' jomp off an de lak',
An' say, " Good-bye, my Rosie dear,
I go drown for your sak'."

Nex' mornin' very early
'Bout ha'f pas' two-t'ree-four—
De captinne-scow—an' de poor Rosie
Was corpses on de shore.
For de win' she blow lak' hurricane,
Bimeby she blow some more,
An' de scow bus' up on Lac St. Pierre
Wan arpent from de shore.

Moral

Now all good wood-scow sailor-men,
Tak' warning by dat storm,
An' go an' marry some nice French girl
An' leev on wan beeg farm.
De win' can blow lak' hurricane,
An' s'pose she blow some more,
You can't get drown' on Lac St. Pierre
So long you stay on shore.

William H. Drummond.

II

The poet achieves his effects not only by the general style of his language, but by his use of particular words. Some words (like some similes and metaphors) have lost their colour by ill-usage: such words as “ nice ”, “ dreadful ”, “ quaint ” and hundreds more. Such words the poet rejects, and uses instead bright living words, words with an atmosphere and a flavour and a background, words that call up clear images and associations in the mind.

In Masefield’s very well-known poem “ Cargoes ” you cannot help but be aware of the rich associations of the words. Compare for instance the vague, unspecific image called up by the term “ ships ”, with the particular and clear-cut associations of “ quinquireme of Nineveh ”, “ stately Spanish galleon ”, “ dirty British coaster ”; and see how much flavour there is to the words the poet chooses to describe the cargoes: there is all the gorgeousness and glamour of the East in:

> . . . a cargo of ivory,
> And apes and peacocks,
> Sandalwood, cedarwood, and sweet white wine.

There is all the wealth and magnificence and colour of the Spanish Main in:

> . . . a cargo of diamonds,
> Emeralds, amethysts,
> Topazes, and cinnamon, and gold moidores.

Contrast these romantic associations with the grimy, sordid, humdrum yet very necessary cargo of the " dirty British coaster ":

> . . . Tyne coal,
> Road-rail, pig-lead,
> Firewood, iron-ware, and cheap tin trays.

Here is the poem:

CARGOES

Quinquireme of Nineveh from distant Ophir
Rowing home to haven in sunny Palestine,
With a cargo of ivory,
And apes and peacocks,
Sandalwood, cedarwood, and sweet white wine.

Stately Spanish galleon coming from the Isthmus,
Dipping through the Tropics by the palm-green shores,
With a cargo of diamonds,
Emeralds, amethysts,
Topazes, and cinnamon, and gold moidores.

Dirty British coaster with a salt-caked smoke stack
Butting through the Channel in the mad March days,
With a cargo of Tyne coal,
Road-rail, pig-lead,
Firewood, iron-ware, and cheap tin trays.

John Masefield.

What a world of romance is revealed by the mere sound of strange, glamorous, musical place-names: de la Mare's " Alulvan ", Newbolt's " Aladore ", and these:

ROMANCE

When I was but thirteen or so
  I went into a golden land,
Chimborazo, Cotopaxi,
  Took me by the hand.

My father died, my brother too,
  They passed like fleeting dreams,
I stood where Popocatapetl
  In the sunlight gleams.

I dimly heard the master's voice
  And boys far-off at play,
Chimborazo, Cotopaxi,
  Had stolen me away.

I walked in a great golden dream
  To and fro from school—
Shining Popocatapetl
  The dusty streets did rule.

I walked home with a gold dark boy,
  And never a word I'd say,
Chimborazo, Cotopaxi,
  Had taken my speech away:

I gazed entranced upon his face
  Fairer than any flower—
O shining Popocatapetl
  It was thy magic hour:

The houses, people, traffic seemed
  Thin fading dreams by day,

Chimborazo, Cotopaxi,
They had stolen my soul away!

W. J. Turner.

Walter de la Mare can work miracles with words. He creates a world of enchantment in which anything may happen, but he does not draw in the details—he simply weaves a magical atmosphere with words. Often it is a sinister atmosphere, and he can make the flesh creep with a single epithet; at witches for instance,

All turning their heads with a smickering smile;

or at the ogre who goes

Whinnying down the dale;

or at the Mocking Fairy

. . . mimbling mambling in the garden.

In his best-known poem " The Listeners " a story is told, not by incidents but by implication. In the following poem, too, the reader is left to supply the details from his imagination:

THE PEDLAR

There came a Pedlar to an evening house;
Sweet Lettice, from her lattice looking down,
Wondered what man he was, so curious
His black hair dangled on his tattered gown:
Then lifts he up his face, with glittering eyes:—
" What will you buy, sweetheart?—Here's honey-comb,

And mottled pippins, and sweet mulberry pies,
Comfits and peaches, snowy cherry bloom,
To keep in water for to make night sweet:
All that you want, sweetheart—come, taste and eat!"

Mocking, yet winsome, knelled that low voice on,
And Lettice looked and listened, sighed and smiled;
Her eyes with lustre lit, her round cheek wan,
Her small heart beating, by such wares beguiled.
Yet in that same small heart a whisper went:—
" Heed not the Stranger and his sugared song!
Only on evil are such pedlars bent:
His sweets are death." Yet, still how she doth long
But just to taste, then shut the lattice tight,
And hide her eyes from the delicious sight!

" What must I pay?" she whispered. " Pay!" says he,
" Pedlar I am who through this wood do roam,
One lock of hair is gold enough for me,
For apple, peach, comfit or honey-comb!"
But from her bough, a drowsy squirrel cried,
" Trust him not, Lettice, trust, oh trust him not!"
And many another woodland tongue beside
Rose softly in the silence—" Trust him not!"
Then cried the Pedlar in a bitter voice,
" What, in the thicket, is this idle noise?"

A late, harsh blackbird smote him with her wings,
As through the glade, dark in the dim, she flew;
Yet still the Pedlar his old burden sings:—
" What, pretty sweetheart, shall I show to you?
Here's orange ribands, here's a string of pearls,
Here's silk of buttercup and pansy glove,
A pin of tortoiseshell for windy curls,
A box of silver, scented sweet with clove:

Come now," he says, with dim and lifted face,
" I pass not often such a lonely place."

" Pluck not a hair!" a hidden rabbit cried,
" With but one hair he'll steal thy heart away,
Then only sorrow shall thy lattice hide:
Go in! all honest pedlars come by day."
There was dead silence in the drowsy wood;
" Here's syrup for to lull sweet maids to sleep;
And bells for dreams, and fairy wine and food
All day thy heart in happiness to keep". . . .
And now she takes the scissors on her thumb:—
" O, then, no more unto my lattice come!"

Sad is the sound of weeping in the wood!
Now only night is where the Pedlar was;
And bleak as frost upon a quickling bud
His magic steals in darkness, O alas!
Why all the summer doth sweet Lettice pine?
And, ere the wheat is ripe, why lies her gold
Hid 'neath fresh new-pluckt sprigs of eglantine?
Why all the morning hath the cuckoo tolled,
Sad to and fro in green and secret ways,
With solemn bells the burden of his days?

And, in the market-place, what man is this
Who wears a loop of gold upon his breast,
Stuck heartwise; and whose glassy flatteries
Take all the townsfolk ere they go to rest
Who come to buy and gossip? Doth his eye
Remember a face lovely in a wood?
O people! hasten, hasten, do not buy
His woeful wares; the bird of grief doth brood
There where his heart should be; and far away
Dew lies on grave-flowers this self-same day.

Walter de la Mare.

In contrast to " The Pedlar " with its lack of clear-cut details, is this picture by Edith Sitwell, sharply drawn and clearly defined; and yet both poems depend on the same thing—the power of words to set up a train of associated images in the mind. Here is the poem:

AUBADE

Jane, Jane,
Tall as a crane,
The morning light creaks down again;

Comb your cockscomb-ragged hair,
Jane, Jane, come down the stair.

Each dull blunt wooden stalactite
Of rain creaks, hardened by the light,

Sounding like an overtone
From some lonely world unknown.

But the creaking empty light
Will never harden into sight,

Will never penetrate your brain
With overtones like the blunt rain.

The light would show (if it could harden)
Eternities of kitchen garden,

Cockscomb flowers that none will pluck,
And wooden flowers that 'gin to cluck,

In the kitchen you must light
Flames as staring, red and white,

As carrots or as turnips, shining
Where the cold dawn light lies whining.

Cockscomb hair on the cold wind
Hangs limp, turns the milk's weak mind. . . .

Jane, Jane,
Tall as a crane,
The morning light creaks down again!

Edith Sitwell.

The poem has the pleasing design of a modern abstract painting. It is all sharp angles and well-defined shapes, and flat, almost crude colour. The images are unconventional and, at first sight, unrelated. The epithets are startling in their incongruity and seeming inconsequence, until it is realized that as the poet's mind moves swiftly from one association to another, the qualities rightfully belonging to one image are transferred to another. All through the poem emphasis is laid on certain verbs and epithets: " creaks ", " harden ", " wooden ", " cockscomb ", as if the poet delighted in playing with these words and arranging them in different combinations.

The associations are obvious. Jane comes down the creaking stair in the cold morning light, and the creaking of the stair is transferred to the light. Her tousled hair standing spikily on end, reminds the poet of a cockscomb, and the same image crops up again in connexion with the jagged-edged petals of the flowers in the garden; then, to make the association sharper still, the flowers " cluck ". The " dull blunt wooden stalactites " of the rain are derived from the banisters as " creaking " is from the stairs. Then, with " kitchen garden " fresh in her mind, the poet appropriately compares the flames of the kitchen fire to carrots and turnips—sharp-pointed orange flames, and the dull rounded rosy glow. And lastly, " whining ", " limp " and " milk-weak " complete the vivid picture of sallow, lanky, untidy, sleepy Jane.

Here is another poem, which, though difficult, and even incomprehensible at a first reading, is easily understood once the mind accepts the associations that the poet's words set up.

THE HOLLOW MEN

A Penny for the Old Guy

I

We are the hollow men
We are the stuffed men
Leaning together
Headpiece filled with straw. Alas!
Our dried voices, when
We whisper together
Are quiet and meaningless
As wind in dried grass
Or rats' feet over broken glass
In our dry cellar.

Shape without form, shade without colour,
Paralysed force, gesture without motion;
Those who have crossed
With direct eyes, to death's other Kingdom
Remember us—if at all—not as lost
Violent souls, but only
As the hollow men
The stuffed men.

II

Eyes I dare not meet in dreams
In death's dream kingdom
These do not appear:
There, the eyes are
Sunlight on a broken column
There, is a tree swinging
And voices are
In the wind's singing
More distant and more solemn
Than a fading star.

Let me be no nearer
In death's dream kingdom
Let me also wear
Such deliberate disguises
Rat's coat, crowskin, crossed staves
In a field
Behaving as the wind behaves
No nearer—

Not that final meeting
In the twilight kingdom.

III

This is the dead land
This is cactus land
Here the stone images
Are raised, here they receive
The supplication of a dead man's hand
Under the twinkle of a fading star.
Is it like this
In death's other kingdom
Waking alone
At the hour when we are
Trembling with tenderness
Lips that would kiss
Form prayers to broken stone.

IV

The eyes are not here
There are no eyes here
In this valley of dying stars
In this hollow valley
This broken jaw of our lost kingdoms.

In this last of meeting places
We grope together
And avoid speech
Gathered on this beach of the tumid river.

Sightless, unless
The eyes reappear
As the perpetual star
Multifoliate rose
Of death's twilight kingdom
The hope only
Of empty men.

V

Here we go round the prickly pear
Prickly pear prickly pear
Here we go round the prickly pear
At five o'clock in the morning.

Between the idea
And the reality
Between the motion
And the act
Falls the Shadow

For Thine is the Kingdom

Between the conception
And the creation
Between the emotion
And the response
Falls the Shadow

Life is very long

Between the desire
And the spasm
Between the potency
And the existence
Between the essence
And the descent
Falls the Shadow

For Thine is the Kingdom

For Thine is
Life is
For Thine is

This is the way the world ends
This is the way the world ends
This is the way the world ends
Not with a bang but a whimper.

T. S. Eliot.

Perhaps this analysis will help to make clear the intention of the poem. Afterwards, read the poem again, and see how much simpler it has become.

Analysis of " The Hollow Men " in Terms of Images and Associations

I

" *A Penny for the Old Guy* " suggests Guy Fawkes' Day and the burning of the Guy, a dummy made of straw and rags. Man is just such a dummy.

" *We are the hollow men, &c.*"—Man of himself is a hollow empty thing; as he goes through life he becomes stuffed with useless knowledge. He cannot stand alone or think for himself.

" *Dried voices* ", " *dried grass* ", " *broken glass* ", " *rats' feet* ".—There is no life in us; even our voices are only sound, all vitality and meaning having gone out of them. Words are a meaningless tinkle. The mention of " rats " adds something hateful and horrible to our lifeless aridity.

" *Shape without form, &c.*"—We achieve nothing: we merely exist.

" *Those who have crossed, &c.*"—The dead do not envy the living—they know we are doomed.

It would be better for us to be damned in doing something—anything—rather than to live out our lives in an utter negation of doing.

II

" *Sunlight on a broken column, &c.*"—Patches of sunlight seem to be the eyes of the dead watching us. We are the broken stone column, warmed by the sun, but in reality finished, useless.

" *Rat's coat, &c.*"—The images suggest a scarecrow. Man is no better than a scarecrow—a thing without life.

III

" *This is the dead land, &c.*"—There is a suggestion of a parched wilderness, a long-deserted land. It conveys the sense that we are dead and useless; that uselessly we pray to gods that are nothing but stone images, as useless as we are; there is no hope in religion or prayer.

" *Death's other kingdom, &c.*"—The world is death's *other* kingdom—the horrible idea that in life we are as good as dead. After death, shall we continue to hope that prayers to useless gods will help us?

IV

" *The eyes are not here, &c.*"—Life and light are disappearing from the world; we are lost souls.

" *In this last of meeting places, &c.*"—There is a suggestion of the spirits of the dead, silent and dumb; we are on the nearer shore of the river bounding the Underworld: we are in the world, yet waiting for that *other* death.

" *Sightless, &c.*"—Perhaps there is still a hope of rebirth in death. In this stanza is the one lovely image in the poem.

V

" *Here we go round the prickly pear, &c.*"—A terrible mockery of gaiety: instead of happy, light-hearted children, we see men, stupidly capering in a meaningless round—a dreadful travesty of gaiety. We are puppets—our movements are meaningless—our life is a stupid endless round, without purpose—we go round and round, getting nowhere, under the delusion that we are living.

" *Between the idea, &c.*"—Man is a failure: he cannot carry his ideas to realization, nor can he achieve more than a gesture of doing; he is doomed by his impotence.

" *For Thine is the Kingdom* ".—It is God who has the power. Man begins something, but wearies before he can carry it through to the end. Life is long—he is weary—his ineffectiveness dogs him. God has the Power; does He keep it from men? Does He make a sport of men?

" *This is the way the world ends, &c.*"—The poem ends on a note of bravado, returning to the nursery rhyme jingle; the old capering starts again—what does it all matter? But we cannot keep it up, the old doubt and fear rises up again, and we end, not with a bang, but a whimper.

T. S. Eliot seems to have no faith or hope in man; or is it not rather, that he has no faith or hope in himself? The poem is full of a dreadful gloom: this is the poetry of introspection: the poet searches his own mind and finds nothing good there. There is something shocking about such complete lack of faith: he condemns the whole world because he condemns himself; the poem is full of pessimism and defeatism.

This is definitely not " everyman's " poetry, because its meaning is not immediately clear. To understand poems like this (and indeed it is good advice for any poem), one should surrender oneself to the mood and the sound, and the impression they make upon the senses and the imagination, without demanding that every detail be supplied and every fact made to fall into place.

That advice needs certainly to be followed when reading the poetry of Gerard Manley Hopkins. He treated words as a poet has every right to treat them, as his material to use as he liked. And he used sounds in the same way, making new words out of them when he could find no existing word to convey his meaning. Here is one of his poems. It is not difficult to understand, once you allow the words to mean just what their sound suggests that they mean. And, let me say it again—the sound will not speak to you unless it is *sounded.*

INVERSNAID

This darksome burn, horseback brown,
His rollrock highroad roaring down,
In coop and in comb the fleece of his foam
Flutes and low to the lake falls home.

A windpuff-bonnet of fáwn-fróth
Turns and twindles over the broth
Of a pool so pitchblack, féll-frówning,
It rounds and rounds Despair to drowning.

Degged with dew, dappled with dew
Are the groins of the braes that the brook treads through,
Wiry heathpacks, flitches of fern,
And the beadbonny ash that sits over the burn.

What would the world be, once bereft
Of wet and of wildness? Let them be left,
O let them be left, wildness and wet;
Long live the weeds and the wilderness yet.

Gerard Manley Hopkins.

There are many strange words here, but they are not incomprehensible. To get as much meaning as possible out of Hopkins' words, one should allow them to set up ripples in the mind—one association leading to another, until one has built up a varied series of complementary images, or has considered and rejected one after the other until the right one is suddenly arrived at. The word " flutes ", for instance, one takes first as a verb, and thinks of it in terms of sound. But after the mind has played about with it, a " fluted " image suggests itself, and one realizes that Hopkins was thinking in terms of shapes, and has invented the verb " flutes " to give shape to the lip of the water as it takes the plunge over the edge of rock. But after the mind has accepted the image, the *sound* persists, and above the roar of tumbling waters, we hear a lighter " fluting ".

" Twindles " is another invention. Listen to the line, and watch what the words are doing:

> Turns and twindles over the broth
> Of a pool . . .

Broth in a cauldron—water swirling in a rock-bound pool—ropes of water falling, turning and twisting as on a spindle—and there is the word, a combination of " twist " and " spindle ".

But even if your ingenuity fail you, you can still enjoy the sound of:

> Degged with dew, dappled with dew;

and of:

> . . . the beadbonny ash that sits over the burn.

" Dappled ", by the way, appears to be Hopkins' favourite word. Just notice how often he uses it.

Here is one more simple poem by Hopkins, and then one for you to puzzle over. In the first (as unconventional as " Inversnaid " in which he praises wet wildernesses) the poet sings of all things that are " pied " or two-coloured—all things mottled or spotted or patched. Notice the association of ideas—try to follow the working of the poet's mind. He goes from "pied" beauty to unusual beauty, the beauty of everyday things. Tools are beautiful because of their fitness for the job they have to do. Then he goes on to the idea that anything unusual—out of the ordinary—unconventional—has a beauty because of its strangeness. He finds beauty in variety and contrast, and finally attributes all beauty to Him who never changes. The words are eloquent and original as always, the alliteration as prodigal and the imagery as compact.

PIED BEAUTY

Glory be to God for dappled things—
  For skies of couple-colour as a brindled cow;
    For rose-moles all in stipple upon trout that swim;
Fresh-firecoal chestnut-falls; finches' wings;
  Landscape plotted and pieced—fold, fallow, and plough;
    And all trades, their gear and tackle and trim.

All things counter, original, spare, strange;
  Whatever is fickle, freckled (who knows how?)
    With swift, slow; sweet, sour; adazzle, dim;
He fathers-forth whose beauty is past change:
        Praise him.

Gerard Manley Hopkins.

And now for one to try your skill on. Before you begin, here is Hopkins himself to advise you. He is not speaking of this particular poem, but his words apply to it as well as to any other:

"Indeed, when . . . I opened and read some lines, as one commonly reads whether prose or verse, with the eyes, so to say, only, it struck me aghast with a kind of raw nakedness and unmitigated violence I was unprepared for: but take breath and read it with the ears, as I always wish to be read, and my verse becomes all right."

And of this poem he wrote:

"The long lines are not rhythm run to seed: everything is weighed and timed in them. Wait till they have taken hold of your ear and you will find it so."

THE LEADEN ECHO AND THE GOLDEN ECHO

(Maidens' Song from St. Winefred's Well)

THE LEADEN ECHO

How to kéep—is there ány any, is there nonesuch, nowhere known some, bow or brooch or braid or brace, láce, latch or catch or key to keep
Back beauty, keep it, beauty, beauty, beauty, . . . from vanishing away?
Ó is there no frowning of these wrinkles, rankèd wrinkles deep,
Dówn? no waving off of these most mournful messengers, still messengers, sad and stealing messengers of grey?
No there's none, there's none, O no there's none,
Nor can you long be, what you now are, called fair,
Do what you may do, what, do what you may,
And wisdom is early to despair:

Be beginning; since, no, nothing can be done
To keep at bay
Age and age's evils, hoar hair,
Ruck and wrinkle, drooping, dying, death's worst, winding sheets, tombs and worms and tumbling to decay;
So be beginning, be beginning to despair.
O there's none; no no no there's none:
Be beginning to despair, to despair,
Despair, despair, despair, despair.

THE GOLDEN ECHO

Spare!
There ís one, yes I have one (Hush there!);
Only not within seeing of the sun,
Not within the singeing of the strong sun,
Tall sun's tingeing, or treacherous the tainting of the earth's air,
Somewhere elsewhere there is ah well where! one,
Óne. Yes I can tell such a key, I do know such a place,
Where whatever's prized and passes of us, everything that's fresh and fast flying of us, seems to us sweet of us and swiftly away with, done away with, undone,
Undone, done with, soon done with, and yet dearly and dangerously sweet
Of us, the wimpled-water-dimpled, not-by-morning-matchèd face,
The flower of beauty, fleece of beauty, too too apt to, ah! to fleet,
Never fleets móre, fastened with the tenderest truth
To its own best being and its loveliness of youth: it is an everlastingness of, O it is an all youth!
Come then, your ways and airs and looks, locks, maiden gear, gallantry and gaiety and grace,

Winning ways, airs innocent, maiden manners, sweet looks, loose locks, long locks, lovelocks, gaygear, going gallant, girlgrace—
Resign them, sign them, seal them, send them, motion them with breath
And with sighs soaring, soaring sighs deliver
Them; beauty-in-the-ghost, deliver it, early now, long before death
Give beauty back, beauty, beauty, beauty, back to God, beauty's self and beauty's giver.
See; not a hair is, not an eyelash, not the least lash lost; every hair
Is, hair of the head, numbered.
Nay, what we had lighthanded left in surly the mere mould
Will have waked and have waxed and have walked with the wind what while we slept,
This side, that side hurling a heavyheaded hundredfold
What while we, while we slumbered.
O then, weary then whý should we tread? O why are we so haggard at the heart, so care-coiled, care-killed, so fagged, so fashed, so cogged, so cumbered,
When the thing we freely fórfeit is kept with fonder a care,
Fonder a care kept than we could have kept it, kept
Far with fonder a care (and we, should have lost it) finer, fonder
A care kept.—Where kept? Do but tell us where kept, where.—
Yonder.—What high as that! We follow, now we follow.—Yonder, yes yonder, yonder,
Yonder.

Gerard Manley Hopkins.

CHAPTER EIGHT

Racehorse or Rocking-horse?

OFF THE GROUND

Three jolly Farmers
Once bet a pound
Each dance the others would
Off the ground.
Out of their coats
They slipped right soon,
And neat and nicesome,
Put each his shoon.
One—Two—Three!—
And away they go,
Not too fast,
And not too slow;
Out from the elm-tree's
Noonday shadow,
Into the sun
And across the meadow.
Past the schoolroom,
With knees well bent
Fingers a-flicking,
They dancing went.
Up sides and over,
And round and round,
They crossed click-clacking,
The Parish bound,

By Tupman's meadow
They did their mile,
Tee-to-tum
On a three-barred stile.
Then straight through Whipham,
Downhill to Week,
Footing it lightsome,
But not too quick,
Up fields to Watchet,
And on through Wye,
Till seven fine churches
They'd seen skip by—
Seven fine churches,
And five old mills,
Farms in the valley,
And sheep on the hills;
Old Man's Acre
And Dead Man's Pool
All left behind,
As they danced through Wool,
And Wool gone by,
Like tops that seem
To spin in sleep
They danced in dream:
Withy—Wellover—
Wassop—Wo—
Like an old clock
Their heels did go.
A league and a league
And a league they went,
And not one weary,
And not one spent.
And lo, and behold!
Past Willow-cum-Leigh
Stretched with its waters

The great green sea.
Says Farmer Bates,
" I puffs and I blows,
What's under the water,
Why, no man knows!"
Says Farmer Giles,
" My wind comes weak,
And a good man drownded
Is far to seek."
But Farmer Turvey,
On twirling toes
Up's with his gaiters,
And in he goes:
Down where the mermaids
Pluck and play
On their twangling harps
In a sea-green day;
Down where the mermaids,
Finned and fair,
Sleek with their combs
Their yellow hair. . . .
Bates and Giles—
On the shingle sat,
Gazing at Turvey's
Floating hat.
But never a ripple
Nor bubble told
Where he was supping
Off plates of gold.
Never an echo
Rilled through the sea
Of the feasting and dancing
And minstrelsy.
They called—called—called:
Came no reply:

Nought but the ripples'
Sandy sigh.
Then glum and silent
They sat instead,
Vacantly brooding
On home and bed,
Till both together
Stood up and said:—
" Us knows not, dreams not,
Where you be,
Turvey, unless
In the deep blue sea;
But axcusing silver—
And it comes most willing—
Here's us two paying
Our forty shilling;
For it's sartin sure, Turvey,
Safe and sound,
You danced us square, Turvey,
Off the ground!"

Walter de la Mare.

I

In the last two chapters we have learnt something of the music of sounds—of ordinary sounds made up from combinations of the twenty-six letters of the alphabet. With them, the poet creates melodies, but:

. . . if he not sing them too
Music they lack.

This extra "singing", lilting quality in poetry comes from rhythm.

All English speech, correctly spoken, has rhythm, which varies according to the arrangement of stressed and unstressed syllables. In ordinary speech the stresses come at irregular intervals, as:

> Hére is the éight o'clock néws for to-dáy, the úmp-téenth of Septémber.

That is Prose Rhythm—irregular, but definite and pleasing. Frequently, however, we find that speech quite naturally slips into a regular rhythm—a Verse Rhythm, as here:

> "I knów you'll cóme if you póssibly cán, but I háve to know définitely éarly in Júne."

That is a piece of ordinary conversational prose, but the eight stresses fall with clockwork regularity. And when we hear the reply:

> "I'll lét you knów befóre the énd of Máy,"

we can only say as Jaques did to Orlando:

> "Nay then, God be wi' you, an you talk in blank verse."

Rhythm is the rise and fall of spoken speech according to the arrangement of stresses, and from Anglo-Saxon times the rhythmical possibilities of language have been exploited by English poets. In the earliest poetry (before A.D. 1000), we find a uniform arrangement of stresses—four to a line—with an indefinite number of unstressed syllables between: speech rhythm in fact, but with this difference, that the lines are meant to be read so that the accents are evenly spaced, even when this necessitates hurrying over groups of unaccented syllables so as to get the next stress in on time. We have the same kind of thing in old ballads and nursery rhymes. For example, in "The Old Woman Who Lived in a Shoe", the lines go swinging along with two stresses each and two unstressed syllables between, until suddenly at the end we have to rush over four unaccented syllables to keep the pace going:

> There wás an old wóman
> Who líved in a shóe,
> She had só many chíldren
> 1 2 3 4
> She dídn't know what to dó.

This represents obviously a primitive stage in verse making, although, as we shall see later, the first of the "modern" poets, Gerard Manley Hopkins, showed what a flexible instrument this old-style verse can become in the hands of a skilled and imaginative poet.

The next stage in the development of English verse came between 1000 and 1400, when the influence of Latin poetry began to discipline rhythm in terms of metre. From the time of Chaucer onward, the principles of Latin quantitative verse (a regular arrangement of long and short vowels) have been adapted to English verse in terms of stressed and unstressed syllables. The line of verse now becomes a unit made up of a number of metrical "feet", metre (or "measure") being exactly the same word which gives us the linear measure of the Metric System. Although on first thoughts its introduction would seem to have clipped the wings of early English free rhythm, the contrary is true, for out of the discipline and restraint that it imposed, has come the poetry of Shakespeare, of Milton, of Keats, of Tennyson—all our magnificent heritage of verse from Chaucer to the present time. Some poets to-day are freeing themselves from its limitations, but one wonders whether this freedom will not destroy much of the music that is the essence of poetry. It is true that metre can be a mechanical sing-song, its accents beaten out with the regularity of a metronome; but when speech rhythm with its flexibility and variety is allied to metre, then the rocking-horse is given life and grace, and freed from its monotonous swing back and forth, it gallops away with vigorous, rhythmical beat, exciting, exhilarating, yet perfectly controlled.

The different feet which form the basis of all traditional English verse reveal their character in their names: Iámb and Tróchee have two syllables of which one (and you see which one) is stressed; the Spóndée has two syllables, both accented; Dáctyl(us), Anapáest and Amphíbrach have three syllables each, of which only one is stressed.

In Latin verse the feet are marked as follows: Ĭāmb (short, long); Trōchĕe (long, short); Spōndēe (long, long); Dācty̆lŭs (long, short, short); Ănă-pāest (short, short, long); Ămphībrăch (short, long, short). In marking the feet in English metres, it is enough to use an accent (′) over the stressed syllable, with (x) denoting the unstressed syllables, only when attention is to be drawn to them.

Examples of words illustrating the different feet are easy to find: "behind", "before", "to-day", "again", are Iambs; "Sunday", "Monday", "Thursday", "Tuesday" are Trochees; "boat-race", "see-saw", "foot-muff", "fireside" are Spondees; "fascinate", "Saturday", "vitamin", "paradise" are Dactyls; "interrupt", "interfere", "overlook", expedite", are Anapaests; and "to-morrow", "emergence", "illumine", "umbrella" are Amphibrachs.

Most people have a keen sense of rhythm, and there are few who have not exercised it in the writing of frivolous or nonsense verses. Stringing together random words in metrical form is quite a good rhythmical exercise, as for example:

Rhododendron, polyanthus,
  Mignonette, geranium,
Gladioli, laurestinus,
  Marigold, chrysanthemum.

If you can rhyme it, all the better; if you can fit it to a tune, better still. This one goes to "Clementine", and if it needs another four lines to fill up the music, here goes:

Tapioca, semolina,
  Custard-powder, gelatine,
Eggs and bacon, mashed potatoes,
  Apple dumplings, margarine.

The poets are not above this kind of fun. Here is John Betjeman enjoying himself with names. You may substitute names of your own, so long as they fit the rhythm: " túmty, túmty, túmty, túmty "; the list can be as long as you wish—in fact you can make your own commination service of it, and bury the bodies in any churchyard you like.

DORSET

Rime Intrinsica, Fontmell Magna, Sturminster Newton and Melbury Bubb,
Whist upon whist upon whist upon whist drive, in Institute, Legion and Social Club.
Horny hands that hold the aces which this morning held the plough
While Tranter Reuben, T. S. Eliot, H. G. Wells and Edith Sitwell lie in Mellstock Churchyard now.

Lord's Day bells from Bingham's Melcombe, Iwerne Minster, Shroton, Plush,
Down the grass between the beeches, mellow in the evening hush.
Gloved the hands that hold the hymn book, which this morning milked the cow
While Tranter Reuben, Mary Borden, Brian Howard and Harold Acton lie in Mellstock Churchyard now.

Light's abode, celestial Salem! Lamps of evening, smelling strong,
Gleaming on the pitch pine waiting almost empty evensong;
From the aisles each window smiles on grave and grass and yew tree bough,
While Tranter Reuben, Gordon Selfridge, Edna Best and Thomas Hardy lie in Mellstock Churchyard now.

John Betjeman.

Poet's Note: " The names in the last lines of these stanzas are not put in out of malice or satire but merely for their euphony.

To return to our serious study of metre: the " foot " most frequently used in English poetry is the Iamb. Out of the poems quoted so far in this book, about two-thirds are in Iambics. Here are some examples:

× / × / × / × /
He gave / a song / a wing / to words.

(4 iambic feet).

^ / × / × / × /
But mark / yon small / green blade / your stones /
× /
between.

(5 iambic feet).

× / × / × / × / × / × / ×
Before / the Ro/man came / to Rye / or out / of Se/vern
/
strode.

(7 iambic feet).

These three lines are perfectly regular, but if you examine the whole of the poems from which they come, you will find that only " The Rolling English Road " is equally regular throughout. Such a lack of variety is usually monotonous, and the sign of an immature versifier, but here the sing-song is perfectly in keeping with the light treatment and rollicking subject.

Usually we find that even when the predominant rhythm is iambic, the poet gives it variety and interest by the substitution here and there of other kinds of feet. Look at the first line of " Nothing is Easy ":

/ × × / × / × /
Nothing / is ea/sy pi/ty then.

This is the commonest substitution of all—a trochee for an iamb in the first foot. It starts off the line on a strong note, whereas the iamb gives a lighter, more lilting beginning.

A more unusual and more striking use of the strong trochaic beat is illustrated in " Beleaguered Cities ". The metre is predominantly iambic, but what about this line:

/ × / × / × / × / ×
Build / your hou/ses build / your hou/ses build / your
/
towns.

By simply omitting the unstressed syllable at the beginning of the line, the poet has given a strong trochaic emphasis to it: he bangs his fist on the table as it were. It is possible, of course, to read this line (and the others like it in the poem) as five and a half trochees (the omission of the weak syllable of the last trochee is common). Try it:

Build your / houses / build your / houses / build your /
towns.

Can your ear detect the difference between the iambic and the trochaic rhythms? Even though exactly the same syllables are stressed, yet the pace of the line is quite different. The iambs move along at a measured, deliberate speed; the trochees prance along light-heartedly, in quite the wrong mood for the strong feeling in the poem.

The iambic line does not always move so heavily. Indeed, it owes its popularity to the fact that it is the most versatile of all metres: it is capable of expressing widely different moods and emotions. With short vowel sounds and crisp consonants it can be made to skip along, while with long vowels and heavy consonants it can sound like a dirge. It is equally suited to the short lines of the ballad metre and to the heroic measure of blank verse; it can suggest the rolling English drunkard as well as three stately barges moving like Empresses down the Thames. It can suggest complete silence and stillness:

> Couched in his kennel like a log
> With paws of silver sleeps the dog;

and it can flash past us with the speed of an express train:

> Out of the silence grows
> An iron thunder—grows, and roars, and sweeps,
> Menacing!

Do you see, by the way, how much that superb climax owes to the sudden substitution in the third line, of a dactyl for the first iamb?

Before we leave iambics, what do you think of the metre of "Morning Express"? Here are the first two lines:

× / × / × / × / × /
Along / the wind/swept plat/form pinched / and white
× / × / × / × / × /
The tra/vellers stand / in pools / of win/try light.

Not much doubt about those, is there? But what about this teaser:

/ × × × / × / × / × /
Boys, indo/lent-eyed, / from bas/kets lean/ing back.

It can be forced into metrical form by making the first foot into a dactyl, but it does not satisfy the ear, because a very strong speech stress pushes its head up on the first syllable of "indolent":

/ / /
Boys indolent-eyed . . .,

and upsets the metre. Here is another line that can be forced into the iambic measure:

× / × / × / × × / × /
Scared peop/le hur/ry, storm/ing the doors / in crowds;

but again a strong speech stress asserts itself on "scáred", and again the line bursts the bonds of metre.

This poem is not made to a set metre, but is written in speech rhythm; and the fact that over and over again it falls into regular iambics, only proves what a close approximation there is between the two. It is because the iambic is so close to speech rhythm, that it is the metre most widely used. And for the same reason, it is only in very bad verse that one finds the metrical stresses cutting across, instead of coinciding with the speech stresses. When this happens the reader must mispronounce or distort the words in order to place the accent as required by the rhythm; or else, the writer, discovering the awkwardness himself, has recourse to clumsy inversions of the normal word order to correct his faulty metre. A certain amount of inversion is allowed, as it is in prose, to give emphasis, or to add grace to the expression; but it must not be overdone. It is permitted, for example, to invert subject and verb:

> Nor sing they forlorn madrigals;

or to invert adjective and noun:

> Nor sing they madrigals forlorn;

but never to stand the sentence on its head and say:

> Nor madrigals forlorn sing they.

If you should come across anything so clumsy, you would be justified in criticizing it, especially in modern poetry, where, because there is such insistence on the language of everyday, any great disturbance of the prose order would strike a wrong note. Here is a modern poem written in iambics, and at the same time in straightforward prose order, with the speech stresses exactly coinciding with the verse stresses:

THE LETTER

He found, within the door,
When he could bring himself to open it,
Lying beneath the slit,
A letter on the floor
Addressed to her: and he recalled how she
Would run so eagerly
At the first clicking of the flap
To find out if mayhap
The post had brought
Her aught;
And how her face would fall
When there for her
Was naught at all.

He stood and did not stir,
With eyes fixed on the dusty envelope,
As though even now, the hope
Of hearing her light footfall in the hall
Behind him were not dead . . .
Then stooping, picked it up, half-feeling she
Must snatch it from him, laughingly—
She, whose quick fire of ecstasy
Was now but ashes in a little urn . . .
And then, unread,
He set a match to it and watched it burn,
When, as the wisp of smoke died in the air
And there was but charred paper left
In his scorched fingers, he
Stood quivering there,
After those long months of numb agony,
Shot with fresh anguish as if new-bereft.

W. W. Gibson.

That is the iambic rhythm then—a rhythm which we adopt almost unconsciously. The Trochaic metre is more restricted, partly because it begins on a strong down beat so to speak, and starts off without any " lead-in ". This gives a very decided and vigorous character to the line—the feet bounce up and down like a ball. Among poems already quoted there are not many written in trochees. " The Grey Squirrel " is one:

/ × / ×
Like a / small grey
/ × /
coffee / pot,
/ × / ×
sits the / squirrel.
/ × /
He is / not
/ × / ×
all he / should be,
/ × / ×
kills by / dozens
/ × /
trees and / eats
× / × / ×
his / red-brown / cousins.

There are some points of interest here. Note, for example, that the full trochaic line ends on an unstressed syllable. This calls for a double (or feminine) rhyme, as: " dozens . . . cousins ". Now feminine rhymes have charm but not much finality, and so we often find the last weak syllable cut off, and half a trochee left to end the line on a strong note as in:

/ × /
coffee-/pot,

and:

/ ×
He is / not.

It is of interest to note, too, that in the second stanza the poet has chosen to carry the final unstressed syllable over to the next line. If he had kept strictly to the metre he would have written:

> / × / ×
> All he / should be,
> / × / ×
> kills by / dozens
> / × / ×
> trees and / eats his
> / × / ×
> red-brown / cousins;

but he carried the " his " of line 3 over into line 4, and so gave an emphasis to " eats " that it would not have had otherwise.

Trochaic metres are very attractive in spite of the fact that they easily become monotonous. The complete trochaic line with its double ending, has the charm of an old acquaintance, as indeed it is; for most of us were fascinated by it and copied it in our school days. It is the metre of " Hiawatha " of course:

> In the land of the Dacotahs
> Lives the Arrow-maker's daughter,
> Minnehaha, Laughing Water,
> Handsomest of all the women.

The poem that follows is a modern example of the Trochee, in its usual form, with the last syllable cut off—a device which gives an iambic cadence to the line. Notice that just as in iambic metres the first foot is frequently changed for a trochee to give strength, so in a trochaic measure an iamb is often substituted for the first trochee to avoid monotony.

Selections from: THE BULL

See an old unhappy bull,
Sick in soul and body both,
Slouching in the undergrowth
Of the forest beautiful,
Banished from the herd he led,
Bulls and cows a thousand head.

. . . .

See him standing dewlap deep
In the rushes at the lake,
Surly, stupid, half asleep,
Waiting for his heart to break
And the birds to join the flies
Feasting at his bloodshot eyes;

. . . .

Dreaming things: of days he spent
With his mother gaunt and lean
In the valley warm and green
Full of baby wonderment,
Blinking out of silly eyes
At a hundred mysteries;

Dreaming over once again
How he wandered with a throng
Of bulls and cows a thousand strong,
Wandered on from plain to plain,
Up the hill and down the dale,
Always at his mother's tail;

. . . .

Dreaming maybe of a day
When her drained and drying paps
Turned him to the sweets and saps,
Richer fountains by the way,

And she left the bull she bore
And he looked to her no more;

And his little frame grew stout,
And his little legs grew strong,
And the way was not so long;
And his little horns came out,
And he played at butting trees
And boulder-stones and tortoises.

Joined a game of knobby skulls
With the youngsters of his year,
All the other little bulls,
Learning both to bruise and bear,
Learning how to stand a shock
Like a little bull of rock.

. . . .

And the gristles of his youth
Hardened in his comely pow,
And he came to fighting growth,
Beat his bull and won his cow,
And flew his tail and trampled off
Past the tallest, vain enough.

And curved about in splendour full
And curved again and snuffed the airs
As who should say Come out who dares!
And all beheld a bull, a Bull,
And knew that here was surely one
That backed for no bull, fearing none.

. . . .

Ralph Hodgson.

Spondees are infrequently used except to give occasional variety; but here is a little poem that illustrates their use:

SCHOOL'S OUT

Gírls scréam,
  Bóys shóut;
Dógs bárk,
  Schóol's óut.

Cats run,
  Horses shy;
Into trees
  Birds fly.

Babes wake
  Open-eyed;
If they can,
  Tramps hide.

Old man,
  Hobble home;
Merry mites,
  Welcome.

W. H. Davies.

Now we come to the three-syllabled feet, and immediately are aware of a quickening of the pace. We have already seen that a line may be speeded up by a succession of short vowel sounds; now we discover that if the number of unaccented syllables be increased without increasing the number of stresses, then the lines go galloping on at a great rate; in other words, the more unstressed syllables there are to the foot, the quicker the line. The Spondee with its two heavy beats and no unaccented syllables is the slowest metre of all, though even this the poet's magic can transfigure to the joyous scurry of " School's Out ". The Trochee and the Iamb can imitate all the motions associated with two-legged creatures: they can walk, dance, skip, hop, run and stroll; but when the four-footed creation comes galloping, it comes with Dactyls and Anapaests and Amphibrachs. It is often difficult (and always unnecessary) to distinguish one from the other—a succession of Dactyls sounding very much like a succession of Anapaests or of Amphibrachs; but we should be aware of the distinctive endings. The Anapaest ends on a strong note; the Dactyl ends on two weak syllables, so that, whereas the Trochee needs a feminine rhyme, the Dactyl is ultra-feminine and calls for a three-syllabled rhyme. Often, however, as with the Trochee, the weak syllables are cut off and the lines end with a stress, thus giving the effect of an anapaestic rhythm. The Amphibrach, of course, ends on an unaccented syllable and calls for a double rhyme.

These " galloping metres " are not suited to purely lyrical treatment as a rule; they have a dash and a gaiety and even sometimes a boisterousness which is out of place in a poem such as this for instance, by Thomas Hardy:

BEENY CLIFF

I

O the opal and the sapphire of that wandering western sea,
And the woman riding high above with bright hair flapping free—
The woman whom I loved so, and who loyally loved me.

II

The pale mews plained below us, and the waves seemed far away
In a nether sky, engrossed in saying their ceaseless babbling say,
As we laughed light-heartedly aloft on that clear-sunned March day.

III

A little cloud then cloaked us, and there flew an irised rain,
And the Atlantic dyed its levels with a dull misfeatured stain,
And then the sun burst out again, and purples prinked the main.

IV

—Still in all its chasmal beauty bulks old Beeny to the sky,
And shall she and I not go there once again now March is nigh,
And the sweet things said in that March say anew there by-and-by?

V

What if still in chasmal beauty looms that wild weird
western shore,
The woman now is—elsewhere—whom the ambling
pony bore,
And nor knows nor cares for Beeny, and will laugh
there nevermore.

Thomas Hardy.

You may read this with seven stresses to a line if you wish, but that gives a monotonous sing-song besides putting stresses on syllables like the last one of the word " loyally "; or you may read it with four stresses, in which case you have three unstressed syllables between the stresses—a metre quicker even than anapaests. I wonder if you feel like criticizing more than the rhythm? Do you find some of the alliteration and assonance unpleasing to the ear?—" flapping free ", " pale mews plained ", " wild weird western shore "; and would you quote as examples of verbal felicity: " engrossed in saying their ceaseless babbling say "?

Here is a poem, however, in which the metre is exactly suited to the subject:

THE WAR SONG OF THE SARACENS

We are they who come faster than fate: we are they who
ride early or late:
We storm at your ivory gate: Pale Kings of the Sunset
beware!
Not on silk nor in samet we lie, not in curtained solemnity
die

Among women who chatter and cry and children who
mumble a prayer.
But we sleep by the ropes of the camp, and we rise
with a shout and we tramp
With the sun or the moon for a lamp, and the spray of
the wind in our hair.

From the lands where the elephants are to the forts of
Merou and Balghar,
Our steel we have brought and our star to shine on the
ruins of Rum.
We have marched from the Indus to Spain, and by God
we will go there again;
We have stood on the shore of the plain where the
Waters of Destiny boom.
A mart of destruction we made at Jalula where men
were afraid,
For death was a difficult trade, and the sword was a
broker of doom;
And the Spear was a Desert Physician, who cured not a
few of ambition,
And drave not a few to perdition with medicine bitter
and strong.

And the shield was a grief to the fool and as bright as a
desolate pool,
And as straight as the rock of Stamboul when their
cavalry thundered along:
For the coward was drowned with the brave when our
battle sheered up like a wave,
And the dead to the desert we gave, and the glory to
God in our song.

James Elroy Flecker.

Those long lines of six anapaestic feet have each a strongly marked pause—a Cæsura. Although the name is borrowed from classical verse, the pause itself was a feature of Anglo-Saxon verse in which every line was strongly divided into two equal parts. This practice persisted into Elizabethan times and spoilt much poetry by the jerkiness and monotony to which it gave rise. Shakespeare, and after him Milton, established the poet's complete freedom to place the cæsura where he wished, or to dispense with it if he felt it to be unnecessary. In lines of fewer than five feet, it is never used. In Flecker's poem its position is strictly regular—it comes in the middle of the line; and the regularity is further emphasized by an internal rhyme. The poem is not long enough for this to make for monotony, and even if it were, the regular gallop would be no more monotonous than the steady rhythm of the galloping hoofs which it so accurately imitates.

In the next poem, too, the metre suggests the galloping of horses, and again there is the long six-foot line; but notice the unusual charm of the short line which alternates with it. Notice, too, that for all the similarity in rhythm, the poem moves along at a less dashing pace than the " War Song "; the phrases are smoother, with a more gracious curve as befits a winged horse flying above the earth. There is no thunder of hoofs except in the line:

> And across the green moat of the drawbridge we foamed
> and we snorted—

appropriately, because that is the only place where

the faery horse sets foot to ground. Can you detect what it is that brings the horse down to earth? It is the sound of the consonants—the explosive " b ", " t ", and " d ", and the friction of the " p " and the " f ".

SUPPOSE

Suppose . . . and suppose that a wild little Horse of Magic
Came cantering out of the sky,
With bridle of silver, and into the saddle I mounted,
To fly—and to fly;

And we stretched up into the air, fleeting on in the sunshine,
A speck in the gleam,
On galloping hoofs, his mane in the wind out-flowing,
In a shadowy stream;

And oh, when, all lone, the gentle star of evening
Came crinkling into the blue,
A magical castle we saw in the air, like a cloud of moonlight,
As onward we flew;

And across the green moat on the drawbridge we foamed and we snorted,
And there was a beautiful Queen
Who smiled at me strangely; and spoke to my wild little Horse too—
A lovely and beautiful Queen;

And she cried with delight—and delight—to her delicate maidens,
" Behold my daughter—my dear!"

And they crowned me with flowers, and then to their
harps sate playing,
Solemn and clear;

And magical cakes and goblets were spread on the table;
And at the window the birds came in;
Hopping along with bright eyes, pecking crumbs from
the platters,
And sipped of the wine;

And splashing up—up to the roof tossed fountains of
crystal;
And Princes in scarlet and green
Shot with their bows and arrows, and kneeled with their
dishes
Of fruits for the Queen;

And we walked in a magical garden with rivers and
bowers,
And my bed was of ivory and gold;
And the Queen breathed soft in my ear a song of en-
chantment—
And I never grew old. . . .

And I never, never came back to the earth, oh, never
and never;
How mother would cry and cry!
There'd be snow on the fields then, and all these sweet
flowers in the winter
Would wither, and die. . . .

Suppose . . . and suppose. . . .

Walter de la Mare.

CHAPTER NINE

Echo Answers

HORNPIPE

Sailors come
To the drum
Out of Babylon;
  Hobby-horses
Foam, the dumb
Sky rhinoceros-glum.

Watched the courses of the breakers' rocking-horses and
  with Glaucis,
Lady Venus on the settee of the horsehair sea!
Where Lord Tennyson in laurels wrote a gloria free
In a borealic iceberg came Victoria; she
Knew Prince Albert's tall memorial took the colours of
  the floreal
And the borealic iceberg; floating on they see
New-risen Madam Venus for whose sake from far
Came the fat and zebra'd emperor from Zanzibar
Where like golden bouquets lay far Asia, Africa, Cathay,
All laid before that shady lady by the fibroid Shah.
Captain Fracasse stout as any water-butt came, stood
With Sir Bacchus both a-drinking the black tarr'd
  grapes' blood
Plucked among the tartan leafage
By the furry wind whose grief age

Could not wither—like a squirrel with a gold star-nut.
Queen Victoria sitting shocked upon the rocking-horse
Of a wave said to the Laureate, " This minx of course
Is as sharp as any lynx and blacker-deeper than the
drinks and quite as
Hot as any hottentot, without remorse!

For the minx,"
Said she,
" And the drinks,
You can see

Are hot as any hottentot and not the goods for me!"

Edith Sitwell.

The Latin influence which gave us metre introduced also rhyme, that attractive echo of similar sound which adds so much to the music of verse. Composition in every artistic medium depends for its unity and balance and emphasis upon a certain amount of repetition, and in poetry the ear delights in it. Even before rhyme was used, early English poetry had its repetitions too in alliteration, a device which has never disappeared although its use has become less obvious, less insistent, and more subtle and restrained. Alliteration overdone can be artificial and sometimes comic; rhyme overdone is jingly and frivolous, but it is always attractive.

Usually it is the last word in a line which carries the rhyme, and the commonest arrangements are: a, a, b, b (rhyming the lines in pairs); or a, b, a, b (rhyming alternate lines); or a, b, c, b (rhyming even lines only). For example:

> Slowly, silently, now the moon — a
> Walks the night in her silver shoon; — a
> This way and that she peers and sees — b
> Silver fruit upon silver trees; — b

or:

> When you destroy a blade of grass, — a
> You poison England at her roots: — b
> Remember no man's foot can pass — a
> Where evermore no green life shoots; — b

or:

> Girls scream — a
> Boys shout: — b
> Dogs bark, — c
> School's out. — b

These represent the normal allowance of rhyme. But, of course, the poet may use a great deal more or a great deal less, or even none at all.

Internal rhyme has the effect of quickening the pace (as we saw in " War Song of the Saracens ") by emphasizing the cæsura and thus giving the impression that there are a series of short lines rhyming a, a, a, b:

> We are they who come faster than *fate*: we are they who ride early or *late*:
> We storm at your ivory *gate*: Pale Kings of the Sunset beware!

That is an obvious use of internal rhyme. But what about Edith Sitwell's " Hornpipe "? There, the rhymes pop up all over the place with great ingenuity—don't miss any of them. Remember that rhymes are intended to catch the ear, and don't simply depend on seeing them.

Rhymes on one syllable only, are direct and strong, and are appropriately called " masculine ". A rhyme on two syllables is lighter, daintier, more frivolous, and therefore—shall we say equally appropriately?—called feminine. When three syllables rhyme, the effect is more than usually frivolous, and unsuited therefore to any but light verse. Edith Sitwell rhymes " benison " with " Lord Tennyson "; and " Victoria " with " memoria(l) " and with " borea(lic) "; and that is good fun. But the fact that one Robert Browning, ingenious rhymester, paired off in cold blood " visit I've " and " inquisitive "; " guarantees " and " arrant ease "; " went trickle " and " ventricle "; " wreathy hop " and " Ethiop "—does not justify Thomas Hardy in doing the same sort of thing in his poem " Night in the Old Home ".

In this poem, the triple rhymes as well as the three-syllabled metre, seem to me quite unsuited to the theme, the treatment, and above all the imagery:

NIGHT IN THE OLD HOME

When the wasting embers redden the chimney breast,
And Life's bare pathway looms like a desert track to me,
And from hall and parlour the living have gone to their
rest,

The perished people who housed them here come back
to me.

They come and seat them around in their mouldy
places,
Now and then bending towards me a glance of wistful-
ness,
A strange upbraiding smile upon all their faces,
And in the bearing of each a passive tristfulness.

" Do you uphold me, lingering and languishing here,
A pale late plant of your once strong stock?" I say to
them;
" A thinker of crooked thoughts upon Life in the sere,
And on That which consigns men to night after showing
the day to them?"

" —O let be the Wherefore! We fevered our years not
thus:
Take of Life what it grants, without question!" they
answer me seemingly.
" Enjoy, suffer, wait: spread the table here freely like
us,
And, satisfied, placid, unfretting, watch Time away
beamingly!"

Thomas Hardy.

On one side of the norm we have had internal rhymes, double and triple rhymes, and all-over-the-place rhymes. On the other side there is half rhyme, assonance, double endings giving the effect of rhyme, and no-shadow-of-a-rhyme-at-all.

Wilfred Owen specialized in half rhymes, ending his lines with words in which the consonants are identical but the vowels are different: as in " leaves " and " loves "; " friends " and " fronds ". In this first poem he uses exact rhymes as well, and intensifies the alliterative effect of his half rhymes by deliberately adding to it:

FROM MY DIARY, JULY 1914

Leaves
    Murmuring by myriads in the shimmering trees.
Lives
    Wakening with wonder in the Pyrenees.
Birds
    Cheerily chirping in the early day.
Bards
    Singing of summer scything thro' the hay.
Bees
    Shaking the heavy dews from bloom and frond.
Boys
    Bursting the surface of the ebony pond.
Flashes
    Of swimmers carving thro' the sparkling cold.
Fleshes
    Gleaming with wetness to the morning gold.
A mead
    Bordered about with warbling water brooks.
A maid
    Laughing the love-laugh with me; proud of looks.
The heat
    Throbbing between the upland and the peak.
Her heart
    Quivering with passion to my pressed cheek.
Braiding
    Of floating flames across the mountain brow.

Brooding
    Of stillness; and a sighing of the bough.
Stirs
    Of leaflets in the gloom; soft petal-showers;
Stars
    Expanding with the starr'd nocturnal flowers.

Wilfred Owen.

In the next the half rhymes are less obvious, but so long as the lines are read with an awareness of the endings, the ear finds enough similarity to satisfy it:

EXPOSURE

Our brains ache, in the merciless iced east winds that knive us. . . .
Wearied we keep awake because the night is silent. . . .
Low, drooping flares confuse our memory of the salient. . . .
Worried by silence, sentries whisper, curious, nervous,
    But nothing happens.

Watching, we hear the mad gusts tugging on the wire,
Like twitching agonies of men among its brambles.
Northward, incessantly, the flickering gunnery rumbles,
Far off, like a dull rumour of some other war.
    What are we doing here?

The poignant misery of dawn begins to grow. . . .
We only know war lasts, rain soaks, and clouds sag stormy.

Dawn massing in the east her melancholy army
Attacks once more in ranks on shivering ranks of gray,
But nothing happens.

Sudden successive flights of bullets streak the silence.
Less deadly than the air that shudders black with snow,
With sidelong flowing flakes that flock, pause, and renew,
We watch them wandering up and down the wind's nonchalance,
But nothing happens.

Pale flakes with fingering stealth come feeling for our faces—
We cringe in holes, back on forgotten dreams, and stare, snow-dazed,
Deep into grassier ditches. So we drowse, sun-dozed,
Littered with blossoms trickling where the blackbird fusses.
Is it that we are dying?

Slowly our ghosts drag home: glimpsing the sunk fires, glozed
With crusted dark-red jewels; crickets jingle there;
For hours the innocent mice rejoice: the house is theirs;
Shutters and doors, all closed: on us the doors are closed,—
We turn back to our dying.

Since we believe not otherwise can kind fires burn;
Nor ever suns smile true on child, or field, or fruit.
For God's invincible spring our love is made afraid;
Therefore, not loath, we lie out here; therefore were born,
For love of God seems dying.

To-night, His frost will fasten on this mud and us,
Shrivelling many hands, puckering foreheads crisp.
The burying-party, picks and shovels in their shaking
grasp,
Pause over half-known faces. All their eyes are ice,
But nothing happens.

Wilfred Owen.

The comic effect of the assonance of Louis MacNeice's poem " Bagpipe Music " is due largely to the feminine endings, and the " Pop Goes the Weasel " rhythm:

From: BAGPIPE MUSIC

It's no go the merrygoround, it's no go the rickshaw,
All we want is a limousine and a ticket for the peepshow.
Their knickers are made of crepe-de-chine, their shoes
are made of python,
Their halls are lined with tiger rugs and their walls with
heads of bison.

John MacDonald found a corpse, put it under the sofa,
Waited till it came to life and hit it with a poker,
Sold its eyes for souvenirs, sold its blood for whiskey,
Kept its bones for dumb-bells to use when he was
fifty.

Louis MacNeice.

Here is another poem in which the attractive double endings give the illusion of rhyme; actual rhyme is used, but only to bind the stanza together.

WINTER NIGHTFALL

The old yellow stucco
Of the time of the Regent
Is flaking and peeling:
The rows of square windows
In the straight yellow building
  Are empty and still;
And the dusty dark evergreens
Guarding the wicket
Are draped with wet cobwebs,
And above this poor wilderness
Toneless and sombre
  Is the flat of the hill.

They said that a colonel
Who long ago died here
Was the last one to live here:
An old retired colonel,
Some Fraser or Murray,
  I don't know his name;
Death came here and summoned him,
And the shells of him vanished
Beyond all speculation;
And silence resumed here,
Silence and emptiness,
  And nobody came.

Was it wet when he lived here,
Were the skies dun and hurrying,
Was the rain so irresolute?
Did he watch the night coming,
Did he shiver at nightfall
  Before he was dead?

Did the wind go so creepily,
Chilly and puffing,
With drops of cold rain in it?
Was the hill's lifted shoulder
So lowering and menacing,
  So dark and so dread?

Did he turn through his doorway
And go to his study,
And light many candles?
And fold in the shutters,
And heap up the fireplace
  To fight off the damps?
And muse on his boyhood,
And wonder if India
Ever was real?
And shut out the loneliness
With pig-sticking memoirs
  And collections of stamps?

Perhaps. But he's gone now,
He and his furniture
Dispersed now for ever;
And the last of his trophies,
Antlers and photographs,
  Heaven knows where.
And there's grass in his gateway,
Grass on his footpath,
Grass on his doorstep;
The garden's grown over,
The well-chain is broken,
  The windows are bare.

And I leave him behind me,
For the straggling, discoloured
Rags of the daylight,
And hills and stone walls
And a rick long forgotten
  Of blackening hay:

The road pale and sticky,
And cart-ruts and nail-marks,
And wind-ruffled puddles,
And the slop of my footsteps
In this desolate country's
  Cadaverous clay.

Sir John Squire.

Unrhymed metrical verse is no new thing of course, for we have had blank verse since Shakespeare's time. Of the poems already quoted, " Ecstasy " by W. J. Turner is a modern example of the poet's ability to give the ear musical satisfaction without the aid of rhyme. Here is another example by Robert Bridges. Steeped in the classical tradition, he was all the same an experimenter with new forms; and in this poem he discards not only rhyme but regular metre, and practically all punctuation:

CHEDDAR PINKS

Mid the squander'd colour
  idling as I lay
Reading the Odyssey
  in my rock-garden

I espied the cluster'd
  tufts of Cheddar pinks
Burgeoning with promise
  of their scented bloom
All the modish motley
  of their bloom to-be
Thrust up in narrow buds
  on the slender stalks
Thronging springing urgent
  hasting (so I thought)
As if they feared to be
  too late for summer—
Like schoolgirls overslept
  waken'd by the bell
Leaping from bed to don
  their muslin dresses
    On a May morning:

Then felt I like to one
  indulging in sin
(Whereto Nature is oft
  a blind accomplice)
Because my aged bones
  so enjoyed the sun
There as I lay along
  idling with my thoughts
Reading an old poet
  while the busy world
Toil'd moil'd fuss'd and scurried
  worried bought and sold
Plotted stole and quarrel'd
  fought and God knows what.
I had forgotten Homer
  dallying with my thoughts

Till I fell to making
these little verses
Communing with the flowers
in my rock-garden
On a May morning.

Robert Bridges.

Reading a poem like that a good many times, and reading many more like it, does, I think, make the ear more sensitive to subtle repetitions and faint echoes, than is possible when the insistent chiming of the rhyme claims and holds our attention. If that is true, then unrhymed verse demands a greater skill in the poet, for as our ear becomes more sensitive we shall expect that the poet who discards one of the most charming features of verse shall create such music in its place, that we are not aware of any loss. The same is true of metre. If he dispense with that too, then he must have an extra felicity of expression lest we regret the abandonment of these two features that four hundred years of poetry have made part and parcel of us.

Now here to end with are two poems which have both rhyme and rhythm, and like the three jolly farmers in de la Mare's poem, they fairly dance each other, and us, off the ground:

THE SONG OF THE JELLICLES

Jellicle Cats come out to-night,
Jellicle Cats come one come all:
The Jellicle Moon is shining bright—
Jellicles come to the Jellicle Ball.

Jellicle Cats are black and white,
Jellicle Cats are rather small;
Jellicle Cats are merry and bright,
And pleasant to hear when they caterwaul.
Jellicle Cats have cheerful faces,
Jellicle Cats have bright black eyes;
They like to practise their airs and graces
And wait for the Jellicle Moon to rise.

Jellicle Cats develop slowly,
Jellicle Cats are not too big;
Jellicle Cats are roly-poly,
They know how to dance a gavotte and a jig.
Until the Jellicle Moon appears
They make their toilette and take their repose:
Jellicles wash behind their ears,
Jellicles dry between their toes.

Jellicle Cats are white and black,
Jellicle Cats are of moderate size;
Jellicles jump like a jumping-jack,
Jellicle Cats have moonlit eyes.
They're quiet enough in the morning hours,
They're quiet enough in the afternoon,
Reserving their terpsichorean powers
To dance by the light of the Jellicle Moon.

Jellicle Cats are black and white,
Jellicle Cats (as I said) are small;
If it happens to be a stormy night
They will practise a caper or two in the hall.
If it happens the sun is shining bright
You would say they had nothing to do at all:
They are resting and saving themselves to be right
For the Jellicle Moon and the Jellicle Ball.

T. S. Eliot.

SKIMBLESHANKS: THE RAILWAY CAT

There's a whisper down the line at 11.39
When the Night Mail's ready to depart,
Saying " Skimble where is Skimble has he gone to hunt
the thimble?
We must find him or the train can't start."
All the guards and all the porters and the station-
master's daughters
They are searching high and low,
Saying " Skimble where is Skimble for unless he's very
nimble
Then the Night Mail just can't go."
At 11.42 then the signal's nearly due
And the passengers are frantic to a man—
Then Skimble will appear and he'll saunter to the rear:
He's been busy in the luggage van!
He gives one flash of his glass-green eyes
And the signal goes " All Clear!"
And we're off at last for the northern part
Of the Northern Hemisphere!

You may say that by and large it is Skimble who's in
charge
Of the Sleeping Car Express.
From the driver and the guards to the bagmen playing
cards
He will supervise them all, more or less.
Down the corridor he paces and examines all the faces
Of the travellers in the First and in the Third;
He establishes control by a regular patrol
And he'd know at once if anything occurred.
He will watch you without winking and he sees what
you are thinking

And it's certain that he doesn't approve
Of hilarity and riot, so the folk are very quiet
When Skimble is about and on the move.
  You can play no pranks with Skimbleshanks!
    He's a Cat that cannot be ignored;
  So nothing goes wrong on the Northern Mail
    When Skimbleshanks is aboard.

Oh it's very pleasant when you have found your little den
With your name written up on the door.
And the berth is very neat with a newly folded sheet
And there's not a speck of dust on the floor.
There is every sort of light—you can make it dark or bright;
There's a handle that you turn to make a breeze.
There's a funny little basin you're supposed to wash your face in
And a crank to shut the window if you sneeze.
Then the guard looks in politely and will ask you very brightly
" Do you like your morning tea weak or strong?"
But Skimble's just behind him and was ready to remind him,
For Skimble won't let anything go wrong.
  And when you creep into your cosy berth
    And pull up the counterpane,
  You ought to reflect that it's very nice
  To know that you won't be bothered by mice—
  You can leave all that to the Railway Cat,
    The Cat of the Railway Train!

In the watches of the night he is always fresh and bright;
Every now and then he has a cup of tea

With perhaps a drop of Scotch while he's keeping on
    the watch,
Only stopping here and there to catch a flea.
You were fast asleep at Crewe and so you never knew
That he was walking up and down the station;
You were sleeping all the while he was busy at Carlisle,
Where he greets the stationmaster with elation.
But you saw him at Dumfries, where he speaks to the
    police
If there's anything they ought to know about:
When you get to Gallowgate there you do not have to
    wait—
For Skimbleshanks will help to get you out!
  He gives you a wave of his long brown tail
    Which says: " I'll see you again!
  You'll meet without fail on the Midnight Mail
    The Cat of the Railway Train."

T. S. Eliot.

CHAPTER TEN

A Matter of Form

PATTERNS

I walk down the garden paths,
And all the daffodils
Are blowing, and the bright blue squills.
I walk down the patterned garden paths
In my stiff, brocaded gown,
With my powdered hair and jewelled fan,
I too am a rare
Pattern. As I wander down
The garden paths.

My dress is richly figured,
And the train
Makes a pink and silver stain
On the gravel, and the thrift
Of the borders.
Just as a plate of current fashion,
Tripping by in high-heeled, ribboned shoes.
Not a softness anywhere about me.
Only whalebone and brocade.
And I sink on a seat in the shade
Of a lime tree. For my passion
Wars against the stiff brocade.
The daffodils and the squills

Flutter in the breeze
As they please.
And I weep;
For the lime tree is in blossom
And one small flower has dropped upon my bosom.

And the plashing of waterdrops
In the marble fountain
Comes down the garden paths.
The dripping never stops.
Underneath my stiffened gown
Is the softness of a woman bathing in a marble basin,
A basin in the midst of hedges grown
So thick, she cannot see her lover hiding,
But she guesses he is near,
And the sliding of the water
Seems the stroking of a dear
Hand upon her.
What is Summer in a fine brocaded gown!
I should like to see it lying in a heap upon the ground.
All the pink and silver crumpled up on the ground.

I would be the pink and silver as I ran along the paths,
And he would stumble after,
Bewildered by my laughter.
I should see the sun flashing from his sword-hilt and
the buckles on his shoes.
I would choose
To lead him in a maze along the patterned paths,
A bright and laughing maze for my heavy-booted lover.
Till he caught me in the shade,
And the buttons of his waistcoat bruised my body as he
clasped me,
Aching, melting, unafraid.
With the shadows of the leaves and the sundrops,

And the plopping of the waterdrops,
All about us in the open afternoon—
I am very like to swoon
With the weight of this brocade,
For the sun sifts through the shade.

Underneath the fallen blossom
In my bosom
Is a letter I have hid.
It was brought to me this morning by a rider from the
Duke.
" Madam, we regret to inform you that Lord Hartwell
Died in action Thursday sennight."
As I read it in the white, morning sunlight,
The letters squirmed like snakes.
" Any answer, Madam?" said my footman.
" No," I told him.
" See that the messenger takes some refreshment.
No, no answer."
And I walked into the garden,
Up and down the patterned paths,
In my stiff, correct brocade.
The blue and yellow flowers stood up proudly in the
sun,
Each one.
I stood upright too,
Held rigid to the pattern
By the stiffness of my gown;
Up and down I walked,
Up and down.

In a month he would have been my husband.
In a month, here, underneath this lime,
We would have broke the pattern;
He for me, and I for him,

He as Colonel, I as Lady,
On this shady seat.
He had a whim
That sunlight carried blessing.
And I answered, " It shall be as you have said."
Now he is dead.

In Summer and in Winter I shall walk
Up and down
The patterned garden paths
In my stiff, brocaded gown.
The squills and daffodils
Will give place to pillared roses, and to asters, and to
snow.
I shall go
Up and down
In my gown.
Gorgeously arrayed,
Boned and stayed.
And the softness of my body will be guarded from
embrace
By each button, hook, and lace.
For the man who should loose me is dead,
Fighting with the Duke in Flanders,
In a pattern called a war.
Christ! What are patterns for?

Amy Lowell.

We are getting perhaps a little nearer to an appreciation of what poetry is and what it is not. We may never arrive at the stage when we can give a conclusive answer to the question: What is poetry? But we can find one reply at any rate to this one: When is poetry not poetry? The answer is: When it is merely verse.

What is verse, then? It is the pattern in which language is arranged so as to please the ear, and the eye too. Instead of writing from one side of the page to the other, line after line, as in prose, the poet prefers to arrange his writing in a series of lines of any length he chooses, and in a shape which is attractive to the eye. The reasons which govern his choice are many: he may cut his text into lines according to a set arrangement of rhymes and rhythm; or he may develop his thought or his picture one idea at a time, giving a line to each; or he may divide his poem according to speech phrases. In any case, the poet pleases himself and he is entitled to make his own design.

But there are certain traditional principles governing all pattern-making, whether in a poem or a wallpaper; and these persist in spite of revolutionaries who would throw them overboard. Progress in the arts consists as much in revealing fresh approaches to old subjects and devising variations on old techniques, as in discovering brand-new subjects and forms; it is certainly not helped by discarding all the past has taught us, and we cannot deny that, willingly or not, we are the heirs of tradition, that the past is present in us, and that we cannot completely unlearn all that we have absorbed from it.

The revolutionary who would turn his back on tradition implies that the past has no value; an obvious fallacy, since nothing can depreciate the treasure it has stored up, no matter how much the present and future may add to it; especially as the present has yet to show its capacity for producing greater painters, poets, musicians and builders than previous ages. By its product it shall be judged: the past " rests ".

Here is one poet, incidentally, who acknowledges his indebtedness:

GRANDEUR OF GHOSTS

When I have heard small talk about great men
I climb to bed; light my two candles; then
Consider what was said; and put aside
What Such-a-one remarked and Someone-else replied.

They have spoken lightly of my deathless friends
(Lamps for my gloom, hands guiding where I stumble),
Quoting, for shallow conversational ends,
What Shelley shrilled, what Blake once wildly muttered. . . .

How can they use such names and be not humble?
I have sat silent; angry at what they uttered.
The dead bequeathed them life; the dead have said
What these can only memorise and mumble.

Siegfried Sassoon.

To return to the poet's pattern in his verse. What are the traditional principles of pattern-making? First there is the element of repetition at regular intervals of identical or similar units; then there is alternation of one motif with another; there is symmetry, which gives perfect balance but which often becomes monotonous; there is balance itself, which is not dependent on symmetry, but which makes possible the endless charm and variety of the asymmetrical. Then there is harmony, which gives unity to the composition; and lest too great harmony prove cloying, there is contrast and occasional discord.

All these principles may be seen in verse. In most poems you will find repetition of identical stanzas; in each stanza you will find repetition or alternation of identical or similar lines, rounded off perhaps with a pair of lines longer or shorter than the rest, and the whole poem centred on the page to look as symmetrical as possible (visual pattern you see, as well as aural). For example:

> If any God should will
> To wipe from mind
> The memory of this ill
> Which is mankind
> In soul and substance now—who would not bless
> Even to tears, His loving-tenderness?

That is what the stanza *looks* like; that is also what it should *sound* like. In speaking verse, the line-endings must be made clear—not always by a pause, but by sustaining the final word, by leaning on it, and lingering on it. Otherwise there is no aural pattern at all.

Rhyme plays a part in dictating pattern. Although

no hard-and-fast rules are laid down, the arrangement of rhymes may be reflected in the shape of the verse on the printed page. A poem written in couplets (that is with the lines rhyming in pairs) is set out with each stanza in a solid block, thus:

a This darksome burn, horseback brown,
a His rollrock highroad roaring down,
b In coop and in comb the fleece of his foam
b Flutes and low to the lake falls home.

With alternate rhymes the second and fourth lines are indented, giving a zigzag edge:

a My mind has thunderstorms
  b That brood for many hours:
c Until they rain me words
  b My thoughts are drooping flowers
c And sulking silent birds.

The pattern of the six-lined stanza quoted above, is dictated by its rhyme-scheme:

  a . . . .
    b . . . .
  a . . . .
    b . . . .
c . . . .
c . . . .

Here is a jolly little poem by Thomas Hardy in which the shape faithfully follows the rhymes:

WEATHERS

I

a This is the weather the cuckoo likes,
b And so do I;
a When showers betumble the chestnut spikes
b And nestlings fly:
c And the little brown nightingale bills his best
c And they sit outside at " The Traveller's Rest ",
c And maids come forth sprig-muslin drest,
c And citizens dream of the south and west
b And so do I.

II

This is the weather the shepherd shuns,
And so do I;
When beeches drip in browns and duns,
And thresh, and ply;
And hill-hid tides throb, throe on throe,
And meadow rivulets overflow,
And drops on gate-bars hang in a row,
And rooks in families homeward go,
And so do I.

Thomas Hardy.

Looking back through the poems already quoted, you will see many pleasing verse shapes following the rhyme pattern. In " Pied Beauty " for instance, the first six lines rhyme: a b c, a b c, and they are set out accordingly:

a Glory be to God for dappled things—
b For skies of couple-colour as a brindled cow;
c For rose-moles all in stipple upon trout that swim;

a Fresh-firecoal chestnut-falls; finches' wings;
b Landscape plotted and pieced—fold, fallow and plough;
c And all trades, their gear and tackle and trim.

Wilfred Owen's poem " From My Diary, 1914 ", shows that the lay-out may add more than an attractive appearance to the verse: the single words, the half-rhymes, standing out from the body of the text, are given a tremendous emphasis—an emphasis which should not be lost when the poem is read aloud.

Visual pattern, then, is a not unimportant factor in making verse attractive and easy to approach. It is not, however, an essential part of the study of verse form.

Metrical verse can be exactly described in terms of kinds of feet, length of lines, arrangement of rhymes and number of stanzas. We have already made the acquaintance of the different kinds of feet, and we have seen how they give their names to the different metres. Length of line is given as one-foot, two-foot, and so on; or more technically, as monometer, dimeter, trimeter, tetrameter, pentameter and hexameter. Sometimes the length is given in terms of syllables: iambic tetrameter, for instance, consists of four feet of two syllables each, and it is therefore octosyllabic. The seven-foot iambic line is called the " Fourteener " after its fourteen syllables.

Monometer is rare, but we have had one example of it in " School's Out " by W. H. Davies:

Girls scream,/
  Boys shout;/
Dogs bark,/
  School's out./

The two-foot line is a gay little measure. We have had an example of Dactylic Dimeter in " Off the Ground " by de la Mare. " The Grey Squirrel " by Humbert Wolfe is written in Trochaic Dimeter:

Like a / small grey/
Coffee / pot.

" A Saxon Song " by V. Sackville-West and " The Bells of Heaven " by Ralph Hodgson are both written in a three-foot metre, the first in trochees and the second in iambs:

'Twould ring / the bells / of Heaven
The wildest peal for years,
If Parson lost his senses
And people came to theirs.

It is not difficult to find examples of the four-foot line, for it is the most frequently used of all; and as the iamb is the commonest foot, it follows that iambic tetrameter is the commonest of all metres:

What is / this life / if full / of care
We have no time to stand and stare.

It is ideal for lyrics, ballads and lighter narrative verse: it is the metre of " The Fish " by Rupert Brooke, of " Miss Thompson Goes Shopping " by Martin Armstrong, and of Masefield's " Reynard the Fox ".

The perfect metre for longer compositions—narrative, epic, poetical drama—is the iambic five-foot (pentameter), the " heroic metre ":

What pass/ing-bells / for these / who die / as cat/tle?

It is indeed the perfect metre without qualification, for it is just as suited to short lyrics as to longer works. It may be rhymed or unrhymed. Rhymed in couplets, it gives us " heroic couplets " as in " Death of a Friar "; it may be rhymed in stanzas, alone as in Yeats' " To the Rose upon the Rood of Time ", or combined with other varieties of line as in Bridges' " North Wind in October "; and it is the metre of the sonnet. Unrhymed it gives us Blank Verse, the metre of Shakespeare's plays and Milton's " Paradise Lost ".

All lines of five feet or more usually have a natural break—the cæsura; and in all save the " heroic " line this break tends to cut the line completely in half. We noticed this in Flecker's " War Song of the Saracens " where the break is accentuated by an internal rhyme. Long lines like this have swing and gaiety and are generally used with three-syllabled metres to suit light and rollicking subjects. There is another six-foot line, however—the iambic hexameter, which has a name of its own—the Alexandrine. It is a stately, dignified line, and is usually found in combination with the iambic pentameter, giving weight and finality as well as variety to the stanza; or you may agree with Alexander Pope, who describes it in his *Essay on Criticism* in two lines of which the second is an Alexandrine:

A needless Alexandrine ends the song,
That, like a wounded snake, drags its slow length along.

A longer line still is the seven-foot line. The "Fourteener" was very popular in Elizabethan days, but it is now considered too sing-song for any but such subjects as Chesterton's "Rolling English Road" to which it is admirably suited. In the extract from Wordsworth's "Star-Gazers" on the other hand, it is quite unsuited to the subject and contributes in no small measure to the triviality of the verses. In modern poetry it is more frequently split up into two or more lines, the commonest version of it being found in Ballad Metre—an octosyllabic (four-foot) line alternating with a three-foot, six-syllabled line. It is the metre of "Nod" by Walter de la Mare, of "Now the Full-Throated Daffodils" by C. Day Lewis, and of the Ballad "Wreck of the *Julie Plante*" by William H. Drummond, and of this:

THE DONKEY

When fishes flew and forests walked
And figs grew upon thorn,
Some moment when the moon was blood
Then surely I was born;

With monstrous head and sickening cry
And ears like errant wings,
The devil's walking parody
On all four-footed things.

The tattered outlaw of the earth,
Of ancient crooked will;
Starve, scourge, deride me: I am dumb,
I keep my secret still.

Fools! For I also had my hour;
One far fierce hour and sweet:
There was a shout about my ears,
And palms before my feet.

G. K. Chesterton.

J. E. Flecker has a fondness for long lines, and in the poem from which the next extract is taken, he uses a line of eight iambic feet. Like his six-foot line, it has an internal rhyme which breaks the line in two and gives the effect (if the speaker of the verse is not careful to keep the line units intact) of a series of tetrameter lines.

From: "GATES OF DAMASCUS"

Postern of Fate, the Desert Gate, Disaster's Cavern, Fort of Fear,
The Portal of Bagdad am I, the Doorway of Diarbekir.

The Persian Dawn with new desires may net the flushing mountain spires:
But my gaunt buttress still rejects the suppliance of those mellow fires.

Pass not beneath, O Caravan, or pass not singing. Have you heard
That silence where the birds are dead yet something pipeth like a bird?

Pass not beneath! Men say there blows in stony deserts
still a rose
But with no scarlet to her leaf—and from whose heart
no perfume flows.

Wilt thou bloom red where she buds pale, thy sister
rose? Wilt thou not fail
When noonday flashes like a flail? Leave nightingale
the caravan!

Pass then, pass all! "Bagdad!" ye Cry, and down the
billows of blue sky
Ye beat the bell that beats to hell, and who shall thrust
ye back? Not I.

The Sun who flashes through the head and paints the
shadows green and red,—
The Sun shall eat thy fleshless dead, O Caravan, O
Caravan!

And one who licks his lips for thirst with fevered eyes
shall face in fear
The palms that wave, the streams that burst, his last
mirage, O Caravan!

And one—the bird-voiced Singing-man—shall fall
behind thee, Caravan!
And God shall meet him in the night, and he shall sing
as best he can.

And one the Bedouin shall slay, and one, sand-stricken
on the way,
Go dark and blind; and one shall say—"How lonely is
the Caravan!"

Pass out beneath, O Caravan, Doom's Caravan, Death's
Caravan!
I had not told ye, fools, so much, save that I heard your
Singing-man.

J. E. Flecker.

Here and there among the stanzas (for there is no rigid uniformity), it is interesting to notice some which accentuate the Persian flavour of the poem, by echoing the rhyme scheme of the " Rubaiyat of Omar Khayyám ". Compare stanzas two, four, six, nine and eleven (taking into account the internal rhymes) with this:

I sometimes think that never blows so red
The Rose as where some buried Cæsar bled;
That every Hyacinth the Garden wears
Dropt in its Lap from some once lovely Head.

Verse form, however, is not merely a matter of shape, or of single lines or groups of lines taken at random, but of definite combinations of lines into stanzas, and of stanzas into whole poems. Just as lines can be exactly described in terms of kinds and number of feet, so certain kinds of stanzas are differentiated. A two-line stanza is a Couplet; a three-line stanza a Tercet, and a four-line stanza a Quatrain. There are a number of longer stanzas with special names, such as the Spenserian stanza, but most are simply extensions of the quatrain, for example:

Tools with the comely names,
Mattock and scythe and spade,

Couth and bitter as flames,
Clean and bowed in the blade,—
A man and his tools make a man and his trade;

and:

See an old unhappy bull,
Sick in soul and body both,
Slouching in the undergrowth
Of the forest beautiful,
Banished from the herd he led,
Bulls and cows a thousand head.

There is of course no end to the patterns that can be evolved. A poet is free to use any number of lines, of any lengths, and with any arrangement of rhymes he may devise. If you look at the first poem in the book, " Nothing is Easy ", you will see that James Stephens has exercised this freedom, and he has made each stanza one line longer than the last, beginning with two lines and ending with seven. The limitations of metre are in truth no limitation at all when one envisages the endless variations that are possible.

Sometimes, however, the poet deliberately sets himself very definite limits, and elects to shape either his stanza or his whole poem in an accepted and fixed form. One of these, which all great poets have loved, is the Sonnet. As first introduced into England from Italy in the sixteenth century, its requirements were absolutely rigid: in this (the Petrarchan form, copied from the Italian poet Petrarch) it must consist of fourteen iambic pentameter lines divided by sense and by rhyme into two parts—the octave (eight lines) and the sestet (six lines). The rhymes are limited to four, or at the most five. In the octave the scheme is rigidly laid down as: a b b a, a b b a; in the sestet some variety is permitted: c d c d c d, or: c d e, c d e. Shakespeare adopted the sonnet but made his own modifications of the form, and so we get the Shakespearean sonnet with its division into three quatrains rhyming alternately, followed by a final rhyming couplet. Milton adopted the Petrarchan form, but did not bind himself to a division of the sense at the end of the octave. All great poets have produced great sonnets, for the limitations of the form seem to have called forth their greatest skill. Modern poets have still further freed themselves from the rigid division into octave and sestet, and have introduced other variations; but the sonnet remains a fixed form of fourteen lines of iambic pentameter.

"Say What You Will" by Edna St. Vincent Millay is a sonnet on the Shakespearean model: the first twelve lines are grouped into fours by sense as well as by rhyme; and the function of the couplet is well illustrated, for it sums up the thought of the poem and says the last word on the subject. Here is another sonnet by the same poet, this time in the Petrarchan manner. The octave rhymes: a b b a, a b b a, and the sestet: c d e, c d e; and there is a definite break at the end of the octave: the octave asks the question, and the sestet supplies the answer:

WHAT'S THIS OF DEATH—

What's this of death, from you who never will die?
Think you the wrist that fashioned you in clay,
The thumb that set the hollow just that way
In your full throat and lidded the long eye
So roundly from the forehead, will let lie
Broken, forgotten, under foot some day
Your unimpeachable body, and so slay
The work he most had been remembered by?
I tell you this: whatever of dust to dust
Goes down, whatever of ashes may return
To its essential self in its own season,
Loveliness such as yours will not be lost,
But, cast in bronze upon his very urn,
Make known him Master, and for what good reason.

E. St. V. Millay.

Wilfred Owen's sonnet " Anthem for Doomed Youth " illustrates the poet's freedom to combine these two modes and to vary them. There is a division into eight and six, but the sestet is not an answer to the octave, but an addition—it poses an additional question and carries on the theme. To mark this division the poet, who rhymes at the beginning in the Shakespearean manner (a b a b, c d c d), changes there to e f f e, and then reverts to the Shakespearean in the final rhyming couplet.

Here is an unusual treatment of two sonnets, put together as four stanzas, in the last two of which the octave and sestet are inverted:

SUCH IS DEATH

I

Saints have adored the lofty soul of you.
Poets have whitened at your high renown.
We stand among the many millions who
Do hourly wait to pass your pathway down.
You, so familiar, once were strange: we tried
To live as of your presence unaware.
But now in every road on every side
We see your straight and steadfast signpost there.

I think it like that signpost in my land
Hoary and tall, which pointed me to go
Upward, into the hills, on the right hand,
Where the mists swim and the winds shriek and blow,
A homeless land and friendless, but a land
I did not know and that I wished to know.

II

Such, such is Death: no triumph: no defeat:
Only an empty pail, a slate rubbed clean,
A merciful putting away of what has been.
And this we know: Death is not Life effete,
Life crushed, the broken pail. We who have seen
So marvellous things know well the end not yet.

Victor and vanquished are a-one in death:
Coward and brave: friend, foe. Ghosts do not say,
"Come, what was your record when you drew breath?"
But a big blot has hid each yesterday
So poor, so manifestly incomplete.
And your bright Promise, withered long and sped,

Is touched; stirs, rises, opens and grows sweet
And blossoms and is you, when you are dead.

Charles Hamilton Sorley.

Another poet used the sonnet form in an unconventional way: in Harold Monro's "Week-End" each stanza is a complete sonnet. All except stanzas IV and IX are strictly Shakespearean. Incidentally notice that the lay-out of each is dictated by its rhyme scheme, and see how stanzas IV and IX advertise their difference. This poem shows, too, that the sonnet is not to be reserved only for grave and dignified subjects; it is proved here to be as light and attractive as any lyrical metre.

And now, here is a sonnet by Gerard Manley Hopkins, so unusual at first sight and hearing as to seem very little like a sonnet; but sonnet it is, and it will serve as a link to carry us on from this study of traditional metres and forms, to modern experiments with free verse and speech rhythms.

"The Windhover" is a sonnet on the regular Petrarchan pattern. It is divided into octave and sestet, and rhymes: a b b a, a b b a, c d c d c d; and since we know that a sonnet must have five stresses in each line, we have a fairly good clue to the reading of it. The poet himself indicates in line twelve, that "sheer" and "plod" must both have a stress; for the rest, we can work it out for ourselves. You remember Hopkins' own advice:

". . . take a breath and read it with the ears, . . . and my verse becomes all right."

THE WINDHOVER

TO CHRIST OUR LORD

a I caught this morning morning's minion, king-
b dom of daylight's dauphin, dapple-dawn-drawn
Falcon, in his riding
b Of the rolling level underneath him steady air,
and striding
a High there, how he rung upon the rein of a
wimpling wing
a In his ecstasy! then off, off forth on swing,
b As a skate's heel sweeps smooth on a bow-bend:
the hurl and gliding
b Rebuffed the big wind. My heart in hiding
a Stirred for a bird,—the achieve of, the mastery of
the thing!

c Brute beauty and valour and act, oh, air, pride,
plume here
d Buckle! AND the fire that breaks from thee
then, a billion
c Times told lovelier, more dangerous, O my
chevalier!

d No wonder of it: shéer plód makes plough
down sillion
c Shine, and blue-bleak embers, ah my dear,
d Fall, gall themselves, and gash gold-vermilion.

Gerard Manley Hopkins.

Before we discuss the form of this poem, notice the dedication of it " To Christ our Lord ", because in that lies the clue to the whole significance of Hopkins' poetry. It is obvious from those of his poems included so far in the anthology—" Inversnaid ", " Pied Beauty ", " The Leaden Echo and the Golden Echo ", and now " The Windhover "—that the poet was as strongly sensitive to beauty as Keats was—beauty that intoxicates the senses until it becomes an anguish in the mind. But unlike Keats, Hopkins' poetry goes beyond mind and sense: it becomes an ecstasy of the spirit, as the poet sees in all earthly beauty the manifestation of the power and love of God.

The sight of the kestrel, first hovering, then swooping in a curve of rhythm more vivid than anything short of the reality could show, fills the poet with admiration of the bird's power and grace. Then in the sestet: if so much beauty and pride and achievement are encompassed in this small body, how much more, how infinitely much more is there in Thee, O God. All creation reflects back Thy beauty—it shines in the freshly turned furrow, it glows in the heart of the falling embers.

In all Hopkins' poetry look for this dedication of beauty to God, and this acclamation of all beauty as being from God.

And now to return to the sonnet. I have indicated the rhyme scheme alongside the poem, to show that its layout follows the Petrarchan arrangement of rhymes, and also to make it obvious that the first line comes to an end on the syllable " king ", that is to say, halfway through the word " kingdom ". The first line can now be scanned as a regular iambic pentameter:

I cáught / this mórn/ing mórn/ing's mí/nion, kíng-/

The next lines are not so simple, but there is no clumsiness nor obvious artifice about them. They are not capable of division into five iambics, but they have the regular five stresses:

-dom of dáylight's dáuphin, dapple-dáwn-drawn Fálcon, in his ríding
Of the rólling lével underneath him stéady aír, and stríding
Hígh there, how he rúng upon the réin of a wímpling wíng.

Born in 1844, Hopkins was no Victorian poet, but was in fact the first of the modern experimenters in rhythm. He did not turn his back on tradition, however, but went farther back than the traditionalists, and in the place of metre, put the Old-English rhythm of stress, with all its copious alliteration, and added to it an equally lavish prodigality of rhyme and assonance. If he is like Keats in his response to beauty, he is like him too in his sensuous delight in sound, in his love of rhyme, and in the inventive skill which enriches his language with hyphenated and newly coined words. Hopkins for some time yet may not be acclaimed as the people's poet. He is a poets' poet, and his influence upon poetry will be a permanent one. It is other poets, inspired by him, who must teach the people to know and to appreciate Hopkins' idiom.

II

It was no new measure that Hopkins used, but he gave it new life and a new name: he called it Sprung

Rhythm. Though it has features in common with both metrical verse and Free Verse, yet it is quite different from either. It resembles metrical verse in that the lines have a number of regularly recurring stresses, but it is incapable of being divided into feet, since it accepts no restrictions as to the number of syllables: we may find four unstressed syllables after the first beat and none at all between the second and third. It is like Free Verse in its rejection of metrical feet and its adoption of speech rhythm, but unlike it in the retention of the regular stress: Free Verse has speech rhythm only, whereas Sprung Rhythm uses speech rhythm and makes of it a pattern.

The inequality in the number of syllables between stresses is balanced and made harmonious by Hopkins' use of speech inflection, of natural pauses, of sustained vowel sounds, of rhyme, assonance and alliteration. When you realize how fond he is of echoes, you will have less difficulty in placing the main stresses.

" Sprung Rhythm " is but one of the departures from strictly metrical form which point the way to " Free Verse ". There are, for example, poems like " Tarantella " and " Wild Broom " in which the poets follow tradition in their adherence to rhyme and to metrical feet, but depart from it in their adoption of lines of irregular lengths. There are poems too, like " Morning Express " and " North Wind in October ", which apparently have an underlying metrical structure, but in which, over and over again, speech rhythm asserts itself and takes charge. Here is another poem by Bridges in which can be seen the influence both of Sprung Rhythm and Speech Rhythm. It is constructed on a basis of iambic pentameter, but the poet, like Hopkins, allows himself liberty to increase the number of syllables—not arbitrarily, but deliberately—to achieve his effects. One line describing the falling snow, particularly illustrates his skill:

/ × × × × / × × × / × × / ×
Stealthily and per/petually / settling and / loosely /
/ ×
lying.

There are four unaccented syllables between the first two stresses, three between the next two, then two, then one, the diminution in the number cleverly following the sense and imitating the motion of the snow—falling swiftly, then gradually settling, and finally lying still. Interwoven with the verse rhythm is a strong speech rhythm, and here and there a word which carries a speech stress but no metrical stress, lifts its head out of the hollow, up to the crest of the wave, as here:

Sílently sífting and véiling *road*, róof and ráiling.

LONDON SNOW

When men were all asleep the snow came flying,
In large white flakes falling on the city brown,
Stealthily and perpetually settling and loosely lying,
Hushing the latest traffic of the drowsy town;
Deadening, muffling, stifling its murmurs failing;

Lazily and incessantly floating down and down:
  Silently sifting and veiling road, roof and railing;
Hiding difference, making unevenness even,
Into angles and crevices softly drifting and sailing.
  All night it fell, and when full inches seven
It lay in the depth of its uncompacted lightness,
The clouds blew off from a high and frosty heaven;
  And all woke earlier for the unaccustomed brightness
Of the winter dawning, the strange unheavenly glare:
The eye marvelled—marvelled at the dazzling whiteness;
  The ear hearkened to the stillness of the solemn air;
No sound of wheel rumbling nor of foot falling,
And the busy morning cries came thin and spare.
  Then boys I heard, as they went to school, calling,
They gathered up the crystal manna to freeze
Their tongues with tasting, their hands with snow-
    balling;
  Or rioted in a drift, plunging up to the knees;
Or peering up from under the white-mossed wonder,
" O look at the trees!" they cried, " O look at the trees!"
  With lessened load a few carts creak and blunder,
Following along the white deserted way,
A country company long dispersed asunder:
  When now already the sun, in pale display
Standing by Paul's high dome, spread forth below
His sparkling beams, and awoke the stir of the day.
  For now doors open, and war is waged with the snow;
And trains of sombre men, past tale of number,
Tread long brown paths, as toward their toil they go:
  But even for them awhile no cares encumber
Their minds diverted; the daily word is unspoken,
The daily thoughts of labour and sorrow slumber
At the sight of the beauty that greets them, for the
    charm they have broken.

Robert Bridges.

Did you notice how skilfully the rhymes are interwoven so as to prevent the poem from falling apart into four-lined stanzas? And can you relate the shape to the rhyme scheme?

Free Verse is certainly " free ", for it admits no restrictions of any kind. It is less certainly " verse ", unless we accept as adequate the view that verse is a mere matter of form. In so far as Free Verse is not set out in prose form, then it is verse. Sometimes you will wonder why the poet did not frankly treat it as prose. In these circumstances you must look to see what, if anything, of attractiveness, of comprehensibility, of emphasis has been gained by the layout. In that lies the poet's justification for his adoption of verse form.

Some Free Verse is rhymed. In the poem " I Have Been Through the Gates ", Charlotte Mew uses rhymed Free Verse. The division into lines follows the development of the thought, each line being one complete image, which calls up that contained in the next line. This evoking of ideas by association is obvious in the last three lines:

His heart is a place with the light gone out, forsaken by great winds and the heavenly rain, unclean, unswept,
Like the heart of the holy city, old, blind, beautiful Jerusalem,
Over which Christ wept.

The stresses are speech stresses, and the lines are rhythmical units and should be read as such, instead of being broken up into speech phrases.

Most Free Verse is made up, not of rhythmical line-units, but of sense-units. The picture is built up one idea at a time, the poet adding just as much as he wants us to assimilate before giving us more, the length of the line depending entirely upon the amount of each instalment—it may be very short, it may be long. The poet places his emphasis by holding up a word or phrase and beginning a new line with it, or by giving it a whole line to itself. The following passage from "The Quails" illustrates this well. First there is the lovely image comparing the birds to the falling petals of a flower; then in the next line the beauty of the picture is shattered by the word "listlessly"; in the next, falling with the birds, we see below them the deadly snare; and then, in a climax of one word, the net receives them. One by one the lines continue the story: the men approach, they disentangle the trapped birds from the meshes of net, they lift in their strong hands the small warm bodies, and in three more lines the birds are dead.

Downward they drift, one by one, like dark petals,
Slowly, listlessly falling
Into the mouth of horror:
The nets . . .
Where men come trampling and crying with bright
    lanterns,
Plucking their weak, entangled claws from the meshes
    of net,
Clutching the soft brown bodies mottled with olive,
Crushing the warm, fluttering flesh, in hands stained
    with blood

Till their quivering hearts are stilled, and the bright
eyes
That are like polished agate, glaze in death.

In " The Pigeon " too the picture is built up one idea at a time. It is almost like a sound film, in which the camera focuses our attention on one point and then leads us to another, the sound track at the same time producing the appropriate accompaniment. In the first line we are shown the concrete-mixer, and we hear it; then we see it " spewing out concrete ". Our eye is then led along the line of the cable to the men operating the machine. Follow the poem through in this way and I think you will agree that the division into lines is perfectly logical.

This principle is applicable to most Free Verse. The division into lines, you see, is not merely governed by the poet's whim. Nor is the division into stanzas an arbitrary one. Look at D. H. Lawrence's poem " Snake " and you will see that the stanzas are as separate and individual as prose paragraphs, and they develop the idea as consecutively.

If you read the next poem with an awareness of the significance of the line- and stanza-divisions, you may find yourself now accepting it as verse:

WORK

There is no point in work
unless it absorbs you
like an absorbing game.

If it doesn't absorb you
if it's never any fun,
don't do it.

When a man goes out into his work
he is alive like a tree in spring,
he is living, not merely working.

When the Hindus weave thin wool into long, long lengths of stuff
With their thin dark hands and their wide dark eyes and their still souls absorbed
they are like slender trees putting forth leaves, a long white web of living leaf,
the tissue they weave,
and they clothe themselves in white as a tree clothes itself in its own foliage.

As with cloth, so with houses, ships, shoes, wagons or cups or loaves.
Men might put them forth as a snail its shell, as a bird that leans
its breast against its nest, to make it round,
as the turnip models his round root, as the bush makes flowers or gooseberries,
putting them forth, not manufacturing them,
and cities might be as once they were, bowers grown out from the busy bodies of people.
And so it will be again, men will smash the machines.

At last, for the sake of clothing himself in his own leaf-like cloth
tissued from his life,
and dwelling in his own bowery house, like a beaver's nibbled mansion

and drinking from cups that came off his fingers like
flowers off their five-fold stem
he will cancel the machines we have got.

D. H. Lawrence.

Here, on the other hand, is a selection which is not verse, but something new in prose:

From PRAIRIE

I was born on the prairie, and the milk of its wheat, the
red of its clover, the eyes of its women, gave me a
song and a slogan.

Here the water went down, the icebergs slid with gravel,
the gaps and the valleys hissed, and the black loam
came, and the yellow sandy loam.
Here between the sheds of the Rocky Mountains and
the Appalachians, here now a morning star fixes a
fire sign over the timber claims and cow pastures,
the corn belt, the cotton belt, the cattle ranches.
Here the grey geese go five hundred miles and back with
a wind under their wings honking the cry for a new
home.
Here I know I will hanker after nothing so much as one
more sunrise or a sky moon of fire doubled to a
river moon of water.
The prairie sings to me in the forenoon and I know in
the night I rest easy in the prairie arms, on the
prairie heart.

. . . .

Out of prairie-brown grass crossed with a streamer of
wigwam smoke—out of a smoke pillar, a blue
promise—out of wild ducks woven in greens and
purples—

Here I saw a city rise and say to the peoples round world: Listen, I am strong, I know what I want.
Out of log houses and stumps—canoes stripped from tree sides—flatboats coaxed with an axe from the timber claims—in the years when the red and the white men met—the houses and streets rose.

A thousand red men cried and went away to new places for corn and women: a million white men came and put up skyscrapers, threw out rails and wires, feelers to the salt sea: now the smokestacks bite the skyline with stub teeth.

. . . .

I am the prairie, mother of men, waiting.
They are mine, the threshing crews eating beefsteak, the farmboys driving steers to the railroad cattle-pens.
They are mine, the crowds of people at a Fourth of July basket picnic, listening to a lawyer read the Declaration of Independence, watching the pin-wheels and Roman candles at night, the young men and women two by two hunting the byepaths and kissing bridges.
They are mine, the horses looking over the fence in the frost of late October saying good-morning to the horses hauling wagons of rutabaga to market.
They are mine, the old zig-zag rail fences, the new barb wire.

. . . .

O prairie girl, be lonely, singing, dreaming, waiting—your lover comes—your child comes—the years creep with toes of April rain on new-turned sod.
O prairie girl, whoever leaves you only crimson poppies to talk with, whoever puts a good-bye kiss on your lips and never comes back—

There is a song deep as the falltime redhaws, long as the layer of black loam we go to, the shine of the morning star over the corn belt, the wave line of dawn up a wheat valley.

. . . .

O prairie mother, I am one of your boys.
I have loved the prairie as a man with a heart shot full of pain over love.
Here I know I will hanker after nothing so much as one more sunrise or a sky moon of fire doubled to a river moon of water.

. . . .

Carl Sandburg.

This is not verse for all its repetitions and parallelisms, for all its layout; but it is something startlingly new in prose. Verse has overstepped the borders of prose and adopted prose rhythms; why should not prose too cross the boundary and turn to its own use the power and emphasis that verse form can add to words?

But these words have power of their own; they have beauty; they have music; they have colour; they are inspired; they are moving;—they are Poetry.

Not all that is verse is Poetry; and not all Poetry is in verse. Verse may be a matter of form, but Poetry is above and beyond all limitations.

CHAPTER ELEVEN

The Question Answered

CRAFTSMEN

From " The Land "

All craftsmen share a knowledge. They have held
Reality down fluttering to a bench;
Cut wood to their own purposes; compelled
The growth of pattern with the patient shuttle;
Drained acres to a trench.
Control is theirs. They have ignored the subtle
Release of spirit from the jail of shape,
They have been concerned with prison, not escape;
Pinioned the fact, and let the rest go free,
And out of need made inadvertent art.
All things designed to play a faithful part
Build up their plain particular poetry.
Tools have their own integrity;
The sneath of scythe curves rightly to the hand,
The hammer knows its balance, knife its edge,
All tools inevitably planned,
Stout friends, with pledge
Of service; with their crotchets too
That masters understand,
And proper character, and separate heart,
But always to their chosen temper true.
—So language, smithied at the common fire,
Grew to its use; as sneath and shank and shaft

Of well-grained wood, nice instrument of craft,
Curve to the simple mould the hands require,
Born of the needs of man.
The poet like the artisan
Works lonely with his tools; picks up each one,
Blunt mallet knowing, and the quick thin blade,
And plane that travels when the hewing's done;
Rejects and chooses; scores a fresh faint line;
Sharpens, intent upon his chiselling;
Bends lower to examine his design,
If it be truly made,
And brings perfection to so slight a thing.
But in the shadows of his working-place,
Dust-moted, dim,
Among the chips and lumber of his trade,
Lifts never his bowed head, a breathing-space
To look upon the world beyond the sill,
The world framed small, in distance, for to him
The world and all its weight are in his will.
Yet in the ecstasy of his rapt mood
There's no retreat his spirit cannot fill,
No distant leagues, no present, and no past,
No essence that his need may not distil,
All pressed into his service, but he knows
Only the immediate care, if that be good;
The little focus that his words enclose;
As the poor joiner, working at his wood,
Knew not the glade from which the trunk was brought,
Knew not the soil in which the roots were fast,
Nor by what centuries of gales the boughs were shaken,
But holds them all beneath his hands at last.

Much goes to little making,—law and skill,
Tradition's usage, each man's separate gift;
Till the slow worker sees that he has wrought

More than he knew of builded truth,
As one who slips through years of youth,
Leaving his young indignant rage,
And finds the years' insensible drift
Brings him achievement with the truce of age.

V. Sackville-West.

I

I have been careful to call this an anthology of "verse", for not all verse is poetry however pleasing or forceful or exciting it may be; in a great deal of good verse you may find a small amount of poetry. For poetry is perfection: it is the product of the divine urge to create, coupled with supreme craftsman's skill.

Poetry is not comparative; its standards are absolute—it is ours that change. We begin by differentiating between good and less good verse; then we find that much we thought good has grown stale by repetition, and we discard it. We go on all our lives, selecting and discarding, but all the time accumulating a store, however small, of poetry which no amount of repetition can stale, of which our ears never weary, whose power to move us never grows less.

But that is a test of time. How can we recognize poetry here and now? Are there any tests which we can apply? Yes, there are; and they may be summed up in a statement of what poetry must be.

A poem must bear the unmistakable mark of

sincerity. It must be inspired by a genuine emotion, some significant experience or some worth-while thought. It must speak from the heart of the poet to the heart of the reader.

The communication must be made in memorable language, which may be simple but never commonplace, which may be erudite but must be clear; and while the poet need not bring his poetry down to the level of the least learned of us, he should be prepared to help the reader where the meaning or implication is obscure.

Poetry must communicate feeling as well as thought: it must have power to move, to stimulate, to excite, to satisfy. It should appeal to the imagination; it should be vivid. It must please the ear with its music of sound and rhythm.

It must have unity: all the elements must be in harmony—treatment, imagery, language and form must be appropriate to the subject and to each other.

A poem must have Beauty; it must have Power. Here is one which for all its simplicity has both. Learn it by heart, for you will never tire of it:

I LOVE ALL BEAUTEOUS THINGS

I love all beauteous things,
  I seek and adore them;
God hath no better praise,
And man in his hasty days
  Is honoured for them.

I too will something make
  And joy in the making;
Although to-morrow it seem
Like the empty words of a dream
  Remembered on waking.

Robert Bridges.

We may not be able to make a poem of our own, but we can, by studying another's, awaken in ourselves emotion and appreciation, and in trying to express both, we can create something.

Let us start then—feet firmly fixed on the ground—choosing a poem that attracts us.

Since poetry is written to be heard, let us listen to it. We must not, however, be guided only by the fact that we like it at a first reading, for that is our instinctive judgment, and it may not be sound. We must examine the poem along the lines we have laid down, and then we shall be able to back up our original estimate with considered judgment.

First—the subject. We must find out what the poem is about, what was the poet's aim in writing it, what inspired him. A great deal of poetry is written in figurative language which must be interpreted before we can get at the kernel of meaning. The subject may be simple and the thought easy to follow; or it may require considerable study before we can elucidate it; or indeed, it may be incomprehensible to us. If the difficulty is due to the complexity of the poet's thought, we have to be prepared to admit that we may not be equal to the poem; but if it seems due to faults of style, or to the writer's failure to express himself clearly, then we may feel justified in criticizing it.

Then—mood and treatment. What emotion stirred the poet? What feeling is he trying to rouse in us? Is he sad, gay, flippant, satirical, serious, dignified, angry, violent, contemplative, contemptuous, ironical? Does he succeed in conveying his emotion to us? Then we ask ourselves if his emotion is genuine and sincere. If the answer is Yes, then it may be a good poem; if the answer is No, if we detect a false note, if the experience seems to be second-hand or the emotion assumed, then it may be good verse, but never good poetry.

Here is another point. We grant the poet absolute freedom of subject, but there are certain moods that are not reconcilable with poetry. Pity for a rabbit in a snare, and anger against a cat that kills song-birds, may seem trivial, but they are expressions of the universal emotion of love. On the other hand, the poet who wrote:

> O why do you walk through the fields in gloves,
> . . . .
> O fat white woman whom nobody loves

was merely giving way to petty, and rather snobbish, irritation. (I wonder why it is that so many poets have this "I wish I loved the Human Race; I wish I loved its silly face" complex? The fat white woman, in spite of her gloves, is superior to inanimate nature and the dumb creation both put together, however little the poet likes her.) But that is by the way. The point for us here is: poetry does not spring from petty personal spite, prejudice and intolerance, but from the universal emotions of love, loyalty, pity, righteous anger, hatred of injustice and cruelty and oppression, from worship of beauty and praise of God.

Now we come to the study of imagery. There may be much of it in the poem we have chosen, or there may be very little; but what there is must be appropriate to the subject and the mood, for an incongruous image can kill the poem by ridicule. We look for similes and metaphors (not a tedious task this, but an interesting and even an exciting one); we say them over and look at the images they call up, and we estimate their accuracy and vividness. We pick out passages of lovely and striking description. And we listen to the effects of sound and try to find out how the poet has created them.

The language must be in harmony with subject, mood and imagery. We look for eloquent words and phrases, for words packed with associations; we are critical of clichés and colourless expressions, and of words that seem to have been chosen because they rhyme or fit the metre and not because they are the best words possible. If we have already decided that the poet's emotion is genuine, and that this may be a good poem, we look now to see if his powers of expression are equal to his inspiration. If they are not, we can pay tribute to the writer's sincerity, but inspiration alone will not make a poem.

Now we listen to the rhythm of the verse, and we are aware of rhyme or lack of it; we know that the poet has used a traditional metre or that he has experimented with a new form; and we ask the same question that we ask at every stage: is it suitable, is it appropriate to the subject, the mood, the treatment and the imagery? If the poet has used a conventional metre, we look for skill in his handling of it: for variety and no monotony, for smoothness and no distortion, and for rhymes that please. If he has discarded metre or rhyme, then we demand that the ear shall be satisfied so that it is aware of no lack of music.

By this time we have come to some conclusions about the poem, and can try to put them into words, to make something of our own, however inadequate. Criticism (and the term includes " appreciation ") is creative to this extent: that it is the product of genuine feeling and sincere study, and—yes—of inspiration. The poet, inspired by God's creation, is allowed to recreate at second-hand, so surely the reader in his turn, inspired by the poet's creation, may be allowed the satisfaction of creating at the third and lowest level; and as God refrains from stooping to smite even the worst of poets, so may we hope that the greatest poets also do no less by us.

You will notice that the simple " appreciations " that follow are planned so that the headings can be discerned: subject, mood and emotion, imagery, language and form—though not necessarily in that order. These give the outline, set down coldly and systematically; but as study gives rise to interest, and interest to enthusiasm, the outline is filled in and coloured. If we take pleasure in our little sketch when it is finished, remember that it springs not from satisfaction at what we have produced, but from a feeling of intimacy with the original poem. While we studied and wrote, we lived with it; now as we read, we live with the recollection of it; we know the poem and we relive our pleasure in it, and we shall never forget it. What poet could ask for more?

My choice falls upon poems about people. Here are two:

IN MERRION SQUARE

On the well-scrubbed wide steps
Of the great house
In the soft summer night
She sits in joyous state,
But still as any pilfering mouse,
Her evening meal laid out meticulously:
Four courses—meat and bread,
Potatoes (cold), and on an old tin plate,
Kept wisely, to await
The waning appetite,
An orange glowing gold.
The rest on paper dishes spread with care,
And as she eats she bows, now here, now there,
With gestures of an old
Forgotten courtesy,
Tempting invisible guests
Out of the purple air,
To share the feast, partake the glowing joy.
O wise ones who pass by

Tell, of your wisdom, tell
Plain truth or paradox
Is it not well
With her alone, not lonely there?
The dish of herbs where love is—
The stalled ox?
Loud guests, lit halls—or silent spirits of the air?

Seumas O'Sullivan.

THE MAD-WOMAN

Aswell within her billowed skirts
  Like a great ship with sails unfurled,
The mad-woman goes gallantly
  Upon the ridges of her world.

With eagle nose and wisps of gray
  She strides upon the westward hills,
Swings her umbrella joyously
  And waves it to the waving mills,

Talking and chuckling as she goes
  Indifferent both to sun and rain,
With all that merry company
  The singing children of her brain.

L. A. G. Strong.

The subject of these two poems is superficially the same: a woman who is harmlessly and picturesquely mad. The thoughts that inspired the two poets are also identical: although the women are out of their minds, they are not poor creatures to be pitied, but happy individuals who are rather to be envied; although they are alone, they are not lonely, but have any amount of company conjured up out of their own imaginations.

The poems are different, however, with the difference between the two women. And this difference is seen, too, in the mood and language of the poems. One is quiet, gentle, wistful; the other is rollicking, gay and full of vitality. One is a study in greys and stillness, the other in bright colours and movement.

The little old lady of Merrion Square sits to eat her supper on the broad white steps of a large house. It is no furtive snatching of a meal from a paper package, but a ceremonious occasion, her meagre supplies laid out on pieces of paper for plates—bread, meat and cold potatoes. The climax to the meal is a lovely big orange (the one touch of bright colour), given a place of honour on an old tin plate, and kept as dessert to the end. She eats daintily, and seeing herself as a hostess at this ceremonious feast, she courteously invites her invisible guests to join her.

She is a tiny trim figure, " still as any pilfering mouse ". She creates no disturbance and makes no litter. She spreads her food out on the clean steps " meticulously ", laying out her meal on " paper dishes spread with care ".

The imagery is as homely and yet as little commonplace as the old lady herself. The language, too, is direct and yet somehow graceful and gracious as the poet describes the old lady presiding at the feast. Then it becomes more formal, more declamatory, almost Biblical in tone, when he addresses the passers-by. He asks them to consider the seeming paradox, that though she is alone, she is not lonely; and he asks which is better: " the dish of herbs where love is " or " the stalled ox "—a feast peopled with real guests, or the company of silent spirits she invokes from the air about her.

The poem is written in rhymed free verse, which is as far removed from the commonplace as the imagery and the language.

The subject of the second poem also, is a woman out of her wits, but with what a difference. There she was a little old lady, quiet, unobtrusive, static. Here she is a vital, joyous, aggressive figure, striding along " the ridges of her world ". Like the prow of a gallant ship, her " eagle nose " juts out pointing her way as she goes " like a great ship with sails unfurled ". In a vivid metaphor she makes her first impact upon us:

> Aswell within her billowed skirts.

The poem is full of gusty movement:

> She strides upon the westward hills,
> Swings her umbrella joyously
> And waves it to the waving mills.

How different from the timid, gracious little figure sitting on the steps in Merrion Square.

But one thing they have in common: both are happy, the one contentedly, the other joyously:

> Talking and chuckling as she goes
> Indifferent both to sun and rain.

Because of their wandering wits, both are more completely happy than most sane people are. For all that they are alone, neither is lonely; for the one has with her the " silent spirits of the air ", and the other:

> All that merry company,
> The singing children of her brain.

Compare with these two poems this one by John Drinkwater. It has exactly the same kind of charm, and the poet is in exactly the same kindly, affectionate mood.

MRS. WILLOW

Mrs. Thomas Willow seems very glum.
Her life, perhaps, is very lonely and hum-drum,
Digging up potatoes, cleaning out the weeds,
Doing the little for a lone woman's needs.
Who was her husband? How long ago?
What does she wonder? What does she know?
Why does she listen over the wall,
Morning and noon-tide and twilight and all,
As though unforgotten were some footfall?

" Good morning, Mrs. Willow." " Good morning, sir,"
Is all the conversation I can get from her.
And her path-stones are white as lilies of the wood,
And she washes this and that till she must be very good.
She sends no letters, and no one calls,
And she doesn't go whispering beyond her walls;
Nothing in her garden is secret, I think—
That's all sun-bright with foxglove and pink.

And she doesn't hover round old cupboards and shelves
As old people do who have buried themselves;
She has no late lamps, and she digs all day
And polishes and plants in a common way,
But glum she is, and she listens now and then
For a footfall, a footfall, a footfall again,
And whether it's hope, or whether it's dread,
Or a poor old fancy in her head,
I shall never be told; it will never be said.

John Drinkwater.

Kindliness, affection and admiration for the homely housewife barricading herself against loneliness is the keynote of yet another poem that we have met already—"Mrs. Hague". It contains a portrait of Mrs. Hague, the gardener's wife, in her simple wisdom and dignity and permanence an integral part of the countryside. The very plants seem ready to twine themselves round her as if she were a tree. She *is* a tree—turned into woman as Daphne was once turned into a laurel. She has guarded herself against loneliness and idleness by planning out her life: the year into its different seasons each with its appropriate activity, the weeks into days each set aside for some special task. And so her days and weeks and years are passed, spent fully, and wisely and happily.

The poet's imagery is full of contrasts: homely imagery contrasts with images suggesting the exquisite flower-bedecked background of a Botticelli picture. The poet's viewpoint is now low, now high. He first sees her above him:

. . . upon a little mound
Of pansies,
Primroses
And primulas.

Or he takes a bird's-eye view of the landscape and sees it as:

. . . this printed muslin beauty
Of clumps and spots and dots and tiger stripes,

an image that suddenly carries us back to the days of our grandmothers and great-grandmothers, and visions of crisp white muslin curtains with polka dots and candy stripes.

In the most striking image of all, he sees Mrs. Hague as a tree:

. . . some old elm had turned to Mrs. Hague,
Thick bole, wide arms and rustic dignity.

So much was she part of the landscape, that the flowers and plants accepted her:

And all the time the primroses, the wind-flowers
Opened their eyes and pressed their nodding heads
Against her, and the moss seemed ready to
Run up those rugged limbs,
The lichen ready
To crystallise its feathery formations
Along these solid branches.

Then quickly returning from a fanciful to a homely image, the poet makes us smell the:

. . . crusty, country odour
Of new bread:

and Mrs. Hague, just now pictured in dignity and sturdiness like an elm, is compared to a contented and placid cow:

> With bovine grace,
> Kind nose, kind eyes,
> Wide open in wide face.

Then the poet's fancy stretches out to find other comparisons that shall adequately describe Mrs. Hague. He is aware of the contrast between her solid bulky figure and her background of ethereal loveliness, and he tries to reconcile the two: it is as if Botticelli, instead of graceful nymphs, had painted Mrs. Noah against his:

> . . . flowering trees, green winds and
> pensive flowers;

or as if Picasso had " inflated " the graceful figure in a Rousseau painting, to the dimensions of one of his abstractionist women.

It is this sense of contrast, almost of incongruity, that fired the poet's imagination.

The language of the poem shows the same contrast. It is exquisite and delicate when referring to:

> . . . the pale blue eye of northern spring;

or when describing Mrs. Hague as:

> . . . seen in summer,
> As through a tapestry,
> Of pool, exotic flower and conifer.

It is homely and colloquial and even has the rustic idiom of Mrs. Hague's speech in:

> Monday was Washing Day,
> Tuesday was Baking Day,
> Wednesday h'Alfred 'as 'is dinner h'early.

The amusing alliteration on " b " in the reference to Sunday, gives that day an extra touch of dignity:

> Black satin bosoms and a brooch,
> A bonnet and a bible.

The very capital letters that the poet uses for " Washing Day " and " Baking Day " and " Strawberry Jam in June " and " Blackberry Jelly in October ", give these days and seasons their due importance in Mrs. Hague's life, and emphasizes the figure in which the poet sees her as having, by the divisions of her life that she has made, planted hedges to enclose her life in its separate departments, and so shut out loneliness.

The poem is written in Free Verse, a medium perfectly suited to the free unconventional treatment; but just as subject, imagery and language are full of contrasts, so is the metre: here and there a rhyme asserts itself charmingly or emphatically:

> Emphatic,
> Rheumatic;

and here and there a line swings along in a rhythm as melodious and regular as any traditional metre:

> . . . Mrs. Hague stood
> Pressed in the narrow framework of her door
> And fills it to our minds for evermore.

Lastly, another poem about a woman—" Mrs. Reece Laughs ". This is just a marvellous description of a fat woman laughing. The poem is built up, as the laughter is, to a terrific climax. The poet is laughing with her, and so are we. She is an enormously fat woman, whose laughter is no mere thing of lips and eyes, but a great convulsion of the whole body.

In the poet's imagery, she is the earth, and her laughter is a tremendous upheaval that begins with rumblings underground. Then follows a mighty storm that shakes the great elms and bends them low. There are more volcanic rumblings underground, increasing in intensity and force, until the inevitable eruption; and suddenly, reverting from the earth to Mrs. Reece, she explodes in " one wild crow " of laughter, her fat arms flung up, her body heaving and straining within its " creaking stays ", her face getting redder, her eyes almost hidden in the folds of flesh. And after this climax, weak with laughter spent, she flops in her chair, fanning her face with her apron.

" And Mrs. Reece has laughed." It is no commonplace or trivial event, but one worthy to be compared with a tremendous cataclysm of Nature. And so, appropriately, the poem is written in language that is far from commonplace. The words resound and reverberate; the language, like her laughter, is " much less simple " than one might expect with such a homely subject. Homely she may be, but her laughter is a world-shattering phenomenon, and must be described in language to suit:

> . . . From hidden sources
> A mustering of blind volcanic forces
> Takes her and shakes her

into " formidable redundancies of mirth ".

The metre is quite regular Iambic Pentameter. The lines rhyme in pairs—they are in fact, appropriately, Heroic Couplets. There is no subtlety, but considerable skill is shown by the poet, first in fitting multi-syllabled words so smoothly into the rhythm of the lines, and secondly, in bringing out rhyme after rhyme as tight and crisp as these are. One internal rhyme is especially effective:

> Takes her and shakes her till she sobs and gapes.

It seems to pick her up, for all her size, and shake her as a terrier does a rat, so helpless is she against the forces that have taken possession of her. She is shaken until she is helpless: with two words " sobs " and " gapes " the poet shows her to us in that awful state of helpless laughter when no sound will come out, and one feels that if the explosion does not come soon, she will burst. Then out it comes, not in an open full-throated bellow, but half-strangled, in a whoop, in " one wild crow ".

The poem is not merely a picture: it has colour and movement. It is not even a talkie in technicolour: Mrs. Reece is alive and real, a person, not a picture. We may be sure that Martin Armstrong has indeed seen Mrs. Reece laugh. And haven't we?

II

Poetry communicates thought and feeling, but often the printed word does not speak urgently enough; the poem needs to be heard, and this calls for one who can, in speaking the verse aloud, interpret and hand on the poet's message. Do you remember?—" In order to speak verse well enough to please ourselves, all we need is the verse. In order to speak it well enough to please other people, we need more of course: an appreciation of rhythm; and sympathy with the poet's aim and emotion . . . the ability to understand and appreciate what we read."

We cannot pass on all that there is in a poem of inspiration and craftsmanship, unless we have taken pains to get from it ourselves—within our limits—all that the poet put into it. The verse to be spoken must be studied and prepared.

First read the poem aloud, beating out the metre with no regard to the sense. Work at the rhythm until you have established it—obviously and with no subtlety. If you fix firmly the basic rhythm at this stage, you will never lose it.

Now study the subject until you understand it well enough to pass it on; you should feel that you can make it easier for the listener to grasp the meaning through his ears, than it was for you to grasp it from the printed page.

You must be able to recognize and share the mood of the poet, so that you speak as though you were he—as though his thoughts and words were yours. Your emotion must be as sincere as the poet's—in fact, of all the qualities that are needed for a speaker of verse, sincerity is by far the most important. Feel the emotion then, and it will express itself in your voice. You must not impersonate the poet and act the part, nor must you declaim the verse; you must simply feel, and then speak as you feel.

Poetry appeals to the imagination, and it is for you, the reader, to build up pictures that your hearers can see, and sounds that they can hear. You can do this only if the images are strongly present in your own mind—if you describe what you yourself are seeing and hearing.

Before presenting a word or a phrase or an image, take care that your listeners are ready and waiting to receive it; pause slightly before and after; isolate it a little; and linger on it as though you loved it. Linger, too, on long vowels and give crispness to the short ones; and bring out the full effect of consonant sounds and alliteration.

Now attend to the speech rhythm, and graft this on to the mechanical metrical basis, which you established so firmly at the beginning, that you do not lose it now, but instead, as the poet did, give it variety, fluency and life.

Rhymes are important, so make sure that they are heard; give them a little extra pressure and let them ring out.

Whatever the verse form, bring out the pattern by marking the ends of lines and stanzas. Your appreciation of the value of the pause (whether it be between speech phrases, or at the ends of lines, or between stanzas; whether it be a silence or only a sustaining of the sound) will make a whole world of difference between your listeners' comfortable assimilation of the poem, phrase by phrase, or their intense irritation and refusal to listen.

Just as there is no such thing as a "poetic language", so there is no such thing as a "poetic voice". Given sincerity and careful speech, the accents of Cumberland or of Cornwall are as pleasing as those of Broadcasting House. All that is banned is slovenly speech, and that you will never be guilty of if you take care of your consonant sounds. Final consonants never sound so distinct to the hearers as they do to the speaker; therefore give an extra crispness to them; and never do in verse speaking what is perfectly allowable in conversation—never commit the crime of making one consonant do duty in two words, ending one and beginning the next.

Now put it all together and practise as you would practise your pianoforte or violin solo, until the whole thing is unified and rhythmical and fluent. If you have a good instrument—a naturally musical voice—then you are fortunate and so is your audience. But do not, whatever your voice, try to exploit its complete range. Poetry should be spoken (though not intoned) with very little inflection.

Do not make the capital mistake of trying to get "the poetry" across. The poet has attended to that; all you have to do is to speak it, as though you enjoy it, with appreciation of its thought, its mood, its imaginative power, its language, rhythm and music. You are both the violin and the violinist; but your listener is not concerned with the study and practice that the violinist has put in beforehand, but only with the sound that is coming from the violin now. Of all that made up your study, only one thing matters now—the sound.

And the moral of that is: Take care of the sounds and the sense will take care of itself.

Among the poems gathered together here are many that make very good speaking and very lovely listening. Here is just one more:

ALL THAT'S PAST

Very old are the woods;
  And the buds that break
Out of the briar's boughs,
  When March winds wake,
So old with their beauty are—
  Oh, no man knows
Through what wild centuries
  Roves back the rose.

Very old are the brooks;
  And the rills that rise
Where snow sleeps cold beneath
  The azure skies
Sing such a history
  Of come and gone,
Their every drop is as wise
  As Solomon.

Very old are we men;
  Our dreams are tales
Told in dim Eden
  By Eve's nightingales;
We wake and whisper awhile,
  But, the day gone by,
Silence and sleep like fields
  Of amaranth lie.

Walter de la Mare.

If in my references just now to " audience " and " hearers " and " listeners ", I have given the impression that this section on the speaking of verse aims at turning out a sort of professional performer, let me correct the impression. The " hearers " I have in mind are sitting, preferably in the singular, on the opposite side of the fireplace, now and then taking a share in the reading; or else they are all round you, mute and so much more attentive, " silent spirits of the air " or " the singing children " of your brain.

And now, quick, before you examine the implications of that last remark, let us go on to the next, and last chapter: " THE POET'S FUN ".

CHAPTER TWELVE

The Poet's Fun

I

There once was a man who said " God
Must think it exceedingly odd
    If he finds that this tree
    Continues to be
When there's no one about in the Quad."

Ronald Knox.

II

Dear Sir,
        Your astonishment's odd:
I am always about in the Quad.
        And that's why the tree
        Will continue to be,
    Since observed by
        Yours faithfully,
                God.

Anon.

This is not a chapter at all, but just a collection of verses showing that the poets, who see things more clearly, and feel things more strongly, and say them more powerfully than we, do not confine their seeing and feeling and saying to serious subjects only. The poets are good company when they are serious; they are excellent company when they are fooling.

If some of the verses you do not understand, don't worry about that; but if you feel that underneath there must be a strong vein of satire if you could only dissect down to it,—forget it! When in doubt, laugh. The creator of Lilliput, if he has followed the adventures of Gulliver in the two hundred years since his (the author's) death, will not be the first, nor the last, to admit that satire is short, laughter long; with the satirist as with the court jester, it pays to be funny, and we will gladly admit even the most disrespectful tilting at our established gods so long as it is good-humoured and witty. The two limericks at the head of this chapter are good examples. So is this:

WHEN SIR BEELZEBUB

When
Sir
Beelzebub called for his syllabub in the hotel in Hell

Where Proserpine first fell,

Blue as the gendarmerie were the waves of the sea,

(Rocking and shocking the bar-maid).

Nobody comes to give him his rum but the
Rim of the sky hippopotamus-glum
Enhances the chances to bless with a benison

Alfred Lord Tennyson crossing the bar laid
With cold vegetation from pale deputations
Of temperance workers (all signed In Memoriam)
Hoping with glory to trip up the Laureate's feet.

(Moving in classical metres). . . .

Like Balaclava, the lava came down from the
Roof, and the sea's blue wooden gendarmerie
Took them in charge while Beelzebub roared for his
rum.
. . . None of them come!

Edith Sitwell.

Here are the rest:

THE WITNESSES

I

You dowagers with Roman noses
Sailing along between banks of roses
well dressed,
You Lords who sit at committee tables
And crack with grooms in riding stables
your father's jest;

Solicitors with poker faces,
And doctors with black bags to cases
hurried,
Reporters coming home at dawn
And heavy bishops on the lawn
by sermons worried;

You stokers lit by furnace-glare,
And you, too, steeple-jacks up there
singing,
You shepherds wind-blown on the ridges,
Tramps leaning over village bridges
your eardrums ringing;

On land, on sea, in field, in town
Attend; Musician put them down,
those trumpets;
Let go, young lover, of her hand
Come forward both of you and stand
as still as limpets

Close as you can and listen well
My companion here is about to tell
a story;
Peter, Pontius Pilate, Paul
Whoever you are, it concerns you all
and human glory.

II

Call him Prince Alpha if you wish
He was born in a palace, his people were swish;
his christening
Was called by the Tatler the event of the year,
All the photographed living were there
and the dead were listening.

You would think I was trying to foozle you
If I told you all that kid could do;
enough
To say he was never afraid of the dark
He climbed all the trees in his pater's park;
his nurse thought him rough,

At school his brilliance was a mystery,
All languages, science, maths and history
he knew;
His style at cricket was simply stunning
At rugger, soccer, hockey, running
and swimming too.

The days went by, he grew mature;
He was a looker you may be sure,
so straight
Old couples cried, " God bless my soul
I thought that man was a telegraph pole "
when he passed their gate.

His eyes were blue as a mountain lake,
He made the hearts of the girls to ache;
he was strong;
He was gay, he was witty, his speaking voice
Sounded as if a large Rolls-Royce
had passed along.

He kissed his dear old mater one day,
He said to her " I'm going away,
good bye."
Nor sword nor terrier by his side
He set off through the world so wide
under the sky.

Where did he travel? Where didn't he travel?
Over the ice and over the gravel
and the sea;
Up the fevered jungle river,
Through haunted forests without a shiver
he wandered free.

What did he do? What didn't he do?
He rescued maidens, overthrew
ten giants
Like factory chimneys, slaughtered dragons,
Though their heads were larger than railway wagons
tamed their defiance.

What happened, what happened? I'm coming to that.
He came to a desert and down he sat
and cried
Above the blue sky arching wide
Two tall rocks as black as pride
on either side.

There on a stone he sat him down
Around the desert stretching brown
like the tide,
Above the blue sky arching wide
Two black rocks on either side
and, O how he cried.

" I thought my strength could know no stemming
But I was foolish as a lemming;
for what
Was I born, was it only to see
I'm as tired of life as life is of me?
let me be forgot.

Children have heard of my every action
It gives me no sort of satisfaction
and why?
Let me get this as clear as I possibly can
No, I am not the truly strong man,
O let me die."

There in the desert all alone
He sat for hours on a long flat stone
and sighed;
Above the blue sky arching wide
Two black rocks on either side,
and then he died.

Now ladies and gentlemen, big and small,
This story of course has a moral;
again
Unless like him you wish to die
Listen, while my friend and I
proceed to explain.

III

What had he done to be treated thus?
If you want to know, he'd offended us:
for yes,
We guard the wells, we're handy with a gun,
We've a very special sense of fun,
we curse and bless.

You are the town, and we are the clock,
We are the guardians of the gate in the rock,
the Two;
On your left, and on your right
In the day, and in the night
we are watching you.

Wiser not to ask just what has occurred
To them that disobeyed our word;
to those
We were the whirlpool, we were the reef,
We were the formal nightmare, grief,
and the unlucky rose.

Climb up the cranes, learn the sailors' words
When the ships from the islands, laden with birds
come in;
Tell you stories of fishing, and other men's wives,
The expansive moments of constricted lives,
in the lighted inn.

By all means say of the peasant youth
" That person there is in the truth "
we're kind
Tire of your little rut and look it,
You have to obey but you don't have to like it
we do not mind:

But do not imagine that we do not know
Or that what you hide with care won't show
at a glance;
Nothing is done, nothing is said
But don't make the mistake of thinking us dead;
I shouldn't dance

For I'm afraid in that case you'll have a fall;
We've been watching you over the garden wall
for hours,
The sky is darkening like a stain,
Something is going to fall like rain
and it won't be flowers.

When the green field comes off like a lid
Revealing what were much better hid,
unpleasant;
And look! behind without a sound
The woods have come up and are standing round
in deadly crescent.

And the bolt is sliding in its groove,
Outside the window is the black remov-
ers' van,
And now with sudden swift emergence
Come the women in dark glasses, the hump-backed surgeons
and the scissor-man.

This might happen any day
So be careful what you say
or do
Be clean, be tidy, oil the lock,
Trim the garden, wind the clock
Remember the Two.

W. H. Auden.

WINE AND WATER

Old Noah he had an ostrich farm and fowls on the largest scale,
He ate his egg with a ladle in an egg-cup big as a pail,
And the soup he took was Elephant Soup and the fish he took was Whale,
But they all were small to the cellar he took when he set out to sail,
And Noah he often said to his wife when he sat down to dine,
" I don't care where the water goes if it doesn't get into the wine."

The cataract of the cliff of heaven fell blinding off the brink
As if it would wash the stars away as suds go down a sink,

The seven heavens came roaring down for the throats
of hell to drink,
And Noah he cocked his eye and said, " It looks like
rain, I think,
The water has drowned the Matterhorn as deep as a
Mendip mine,
But I don't care where the water goes if it doesn't get
into the wine."

But Noah he sinned, and we have sinned; on tipsy feet
we trod,
Till a great big black teetotaller was sent to us for a rod,
And you can't get wine at a P.S.A., or chapel, or
Eisteddfod,
But the Curse of Water has come again because of the
wrath of God,
And water is on the Bishop's board and the Higher
Thinker's shrine,
But I don't care where the water goes if it doesn't get
into the wine.

G. K. Chesterton.

the old trouper

i ran onto mehitabel again
last evening
she is inhabiting
a decayed trunk
which lies in an alley
in greenwich village
in company with the
most villainous tom cat
i have ever seen

but there is nothing
wrong about the association
archy she told me
it is merely a plutonic
attachment
and the thing can be
believed for the tom
looks like one of pluto s demons
it is a theatre trunk
archy mehitabel told me
and tom is an old theatre cat
he has given his life
to the theatre
he claims that richard
mansfield once
kicked him out of the way
and then cried because
he had done it and
petted him
and at another time
he says in a case
of emergency
he played a bloodhound
in a production of
uncle tom s cabin
the stage is not what it
used to be tom says
he puts his front paw
on his breast and says
they don t have it any more
they don t have it here
the old troupers are gone
there s nobody can troupe
any more
they are all amateurs nowadays

they haven t got it
here
there are only
five or six of us oldtime
troupers left
this generation does not know
what stage presence is
personality is what they lack
personality
where would they get
the training my old friends
got in the stock companies
i knew mr booth very well
says tom
and a law should be passed
preventing anybody else
from ever playing
in any play he ever
played in
there was a trouper for you
i used to sit on his knee
and purr when i was
a kitten he used to tell me
how much he valued my opinion
finish is what they lack
finish
and they haven t got it
here
and again he laid his paw
on his breast
i remember mr daly very
well too
i was with mr daly s company
for several years
there was art for you

there was team work
there was direction
they knew the theatre
and they all had it
here
for two years mr daly
would not ring up the curtain
unless i was in the
prompter s box
they are amateurs nowadays
rank amateurs all of them
for two seasons i played
the dog in joseph
jefferson s rip van winkle
it is true i never came
on the stage
but he knew i was just off
and it helped him
i would like to see
one of your modern
theatre cats
act a dog so well
that would convince
a trouper like jo jefferson
but they haven t got it
nowadays
they haven t got it
here
jo jefferson had it he had it
here
i come of a long line
of theatre cats
my grandfather
was with forrest
he had it he was a real trouper

my grandfather said
he had a voice
that used to shake
the ferryboats
on the north river
once he lost his beard
and my grandfather
dropped from the
fly gallery and landed
under his chin
and played his beard
for the rest of the act
you don t see any theatre
cat that could do that
nowadays
they haven t got it they
haven t got it
here
once i played the owl
in modjeska s production
of macbeth
i sat above the castle gate
in the murder scene
and made my yellow
eyes shine through the dusk
like an owl s eyes
modjeska was a real
trouper she knew how to pick
her support i would like
to see any of these modern
theatre cats play the owl s eyes
to modjeska s lady macbeth
but they haven t got it nowadays
they haven t got it
here

mehitabel he says
both our professions
are being ruined
by amateurs

archy

Don Marquis.

(archy by the way is a cockroach, and his inability to press down the Shift Key on the typewriter, is responsible for his shortage of capitals and punctuation.)

CAPE HORN GOSPEL

I

" I was in a hooker once," said Karlssen,
" And Bill, as was a seaman, died,
So we lashed him in an old tarpaulin
And tumbled him across the side;
And the fun of it was that all his gear was
Divided up among the crew
Before that blushing human error,
Our crawling little captain, knew.

" On the passage home one morning
(As certain as I prays for grace)
There was old Bill's shadder a-hauling
At the weather mizzen-topsail brace.
He was all grown green with sea-weed,
He was all lashed up and shored;
So I says to him, I says, ' Why, Billy!
What's a-bringin' of you back aboard?'

" ' I'm a-weary of them there mermaids,'
Says old Bill's ghost to me;

' It ain't no place there for a Christian
Below there—under the sea.
For it's all blown sand and shipwrecks,
And old bones eaten bare,
And them cold fishy females
With long green weeds for hair.

" ' And there ain't no dances shuffled,
And no old yarns is spun,
And there ain't no stars but starfish,
And never any moon or sun.
I heard your keel a-passing
And the running rattle of the brace,'
And he says ' Stand by,' says William,
' For a shift towards a better place.'

" Well, he sogered about decks till sunrise,
When a rooster in the hen-coop crowed,
And as so much smoke he faded
And as so much smoke he goed;
And I've often wondered since, Jan,
How his old ghost stands to fare
Long o' them cold fishy females
With long green weeds for hair."

John Masefield.

SOUVENIR DE MONSIEUR POOP

I am the self-appointed guardian of English literature,
I believe tremendously in the significance of age;
I believe that a writer is wise at 50,
Ten years wiser at 60, at 70 a sage.
I believe that juniors are lively, to be encouraged with
discretion and snubbed,

I believe also that they are bouncing, communistic, ill-
mannered and, of course, young.
But I never define what I mean by youth
Because the word undefined is more useful for general
purposes of abuse.
I believe that literature is a school where only those who
apply themselves diligently to their tasks acquire
merit.
And only they after the passage of a good many years
(see above),
But then I am an old fogey.
I always write more in sorrow than in anger,
I am, after all, devoted to Shakespeare, Milton,
And, coming to our own times,
Of course
Housman.
I have never been known to say a word against the
established classics,
I am in fact devoted to the established classics.

In the service of literature I believe absolutely in the
principle of division;
I divide into age groups and also into schools.
This is in keeping with my scholastic mind, and enables
me to trounce
Not only youth
(Which might be thought intellectually frivolous by
pedants) but also periodical tendencies,
To ventilate, in a word, my own political and moral
philosophy.
(When I say that I am an old fogey, I am, of course,
joking.)
English literature, as I see it, requires to be defended
By a person of integrity and essential good humour

Against the forces of fanaticism, idiosyncrasy and anarchy.
I perfectly apprehend the perilous nature of my convictions
And I am prepared to go to the stake
For Shakespeare, Milton,
And, coming to our own times,
Of course
Housman.
I cannot say more than that, can I?
And I do not deem it advisable, in the interests of the editor to whom I am spatially contracted
To say less.

Stevie Smith.

POPULAR SONG

For Constant Lambert

Lily O'Grady,
Silly and shady,
Longing to be
A lazy lady,
Walked by the cupolas, gables in the
Lake's Georgian stables,
In a fairy tale like the heat intense,
And the mist in the woods when across the fence
The children gathering strawberries
Are changed by the heat into negresses,
Though their fair hair
Shines there
Like gold-haired planets, Calliope, Io,
Pomona, Antiope, Echo, and Clio.
Then Lily O'Grady,
Silly and shady,

Sauntered along like a
Lazy lady:
Beside the waves' haycocks her gown with tucks
Was of satin the colour of shining green ducks,
And her fol-de-rol
Parasol
Was a great gold sun o'er the haycocks shining,
But she was a negress black as the shade
That time on the brightest lady laid,
Then a satyr, dog-haired as trunks of trees,
Began to flatter, began to tease,
And she ran like the nymphs with golden foot
That trampled the strawberry, buttercup root,
In the thick gold dew as bright as the mesh
Of dead Panope's golden flesh,
Made from the music whence were born
Memphis and Thebes in the first hot morn,
—And ran, to wake
In the lake,
Where the water-ripples seem hay to rake.
And Charlottine,
Adeline,
Round rose-bubbling Victorine,
And the other fish
Express a wish
For mastic mantles and gowns with a swish;
And bright and slight as the posies
Of buttercups and of roses,
And buds of the wild wood-lilies
They chase her, as frisky as fillies.
The red retriever-haired satyr
Can whine and tease her and flatter,
But Lily O'Grady,
Silly and shady,
In the deep shade is a lazy lady;

Now Pompey's dead, Homer's read,
Heliogabalus lost his head,
And shade is on the brightest wing,
And dust forbids the bird to sing.

Edith Sitwell.

THE SHIP OF RIO

There was a ship of Rio
  Sailed out into the blue,
And nine and ninety monkeys
  Were all her jovial crew.
From bo'sun to the cabin boy,
  From quarter to caboose,
There weren't a stitch of calico
  To breech 'em—tight or loose;
From spar to deck, from deck to keel,
  From barnacle to shroud,
There weren't one pair of reach-me-downs
  To all that jabbering crowd.
But wasn't it a gladsome sight,
  When roared the deep-sea gales,
To see them reef her fore and aft,
  A-swinging by their tails!
Oh, wasn't it a gladsome sight,
  When glassy calm did come,
To see them squatting tailor-wise
  Around a keg of rum!
Oh, wasn't it a gladsome sight,
  When in she sailed to land,
To see them all a-scampering skip
  For nuts across the sand!

Walter de la Mare.

ROMAN WALL BLUES

Over the heather the wet wind blows,
I've lice in my tunic and a cold in my nose.

The rain comes pattering out of the sky,
I'm a Wall soldier, I don't know why.

The mist creeps over the hard grey stone,
My girl's in Tungria; I sleep alone.

Aulus goes hanging round her place,
I don't like his manners, I don't like his face.

Piso's a Christian, he worships a fish;
There'd be no kissing if he had his wish.

She gave me a ring but I diced it away;
I want my girl and I want my pay.

When I'm a veteran with only one eye
I shall do nothing but look at the sky.

W. H. Auden.

DUCKS

I

From troubles of the world
I turn to ducks,
Beautiful comical things
Sleeping or curled
Their heads beneath white wings

By water cool,
Or finding curious things
To eat in various mucks
Beneath the pool,
Tails uppermost, or waddling
Sailor-like on the shores
Of ponds, or paddling
—Left! right!—with fanlike feet
Which are for steady oars
When they (white galleys) float
Each bird a boat
Rippling at will the sweet
Wide waterway. . . .
When night is fallen *you* creep
Upstairs, but drakes and dillies
Nest with pale water-stars,
Moonbeams and shadow bars,
And water-lilies:
Fearful too much to sleep
Since they've no locks
To click against the teeth
Of weasel and fox.
And warm beneath
Are eggs of cloudy green
Whence hungry rats and lean
Would stealthily suck
New life, but for the mien,
The bold ferocious mien
Of the mother-duck.

II

Yes, ducks are valiant things
On nests of twigs and straws,
And ducks are soothy things

And lovely on the lake
When that the sunlight draws
Thereon their pictures dim
In colours cool.
And when beneath the pool
They dabble, and when they swim
And make their rippling rings,
O ducks are beautiful things!

But ducks are comical things:—
As comical as you.
Quack!
They waddle round, they do.
They eat all sorts of things,
And then they quack.
By barn and stable and stack
They wander at their will,
But if you go too near
They look at you through black
Small topaz-tinted eyes
And wish you ill.
Triangular and clear
They leave their curious track
In mud at the water's edge,
And there amid the sedge
And slime they gobble and peer
Saying "Quack! quack!"

III

When God had finished the stars and whirl of coloured
suns
He turned His mind from big things to fashion little
ones,
Beautiful tiny things (like daisies) He made, and then

He made the comical ones in case the minds of men
Should stiffen and become
Dull, humourless and glum:
And so forgetful of their Maker be
As to take even themselves—*quite seriously.*
Caterpillars and cats are lively and excellent puns:
All God's jokes are good—even the practical ones!
And as for the duck, I think God must have smiled a bit
Seeing those bright eyes blink on the day He fashioned it.
And He's probably laughing still at the sound that came out of its bill!

F. W. Harvey.

INDEX OF AUTHORS